Ivonne Delaflor's book, *India, the Journey of a Lifetime,* is the record of a sincere seeker from a completely different culture discovering the mystery and magic and rigors of encountering authentic spiritual people in India. Her joy in her journey and her endless optimism are inspiring to anyone contemplating a journey into Indian religion and spirituality.

**Swami Chetanananda**
**www.chetanananda.org**

India is a land of many opportunities, inner awakening included. Ms. Ivonne Delaflor describes her spiritual journey in India both vividly and beautifully. May everyone derive the benefit of her insight through reading *India: The Journey of a Lifetime*.

Namah Shivaya,
~ Br. Dayamrita Chaitanya
M.A.Center
www.ammachi.org

India; it's indeed a Journey of a lifetime, and a timely message of hope and love especially for all those affected with the Tsunami in India. I believe this book will deliver strength and trust that INDIA has divine protection to arise and heal, and the necessary power to believe in its own magic.

—Swami Ramananda

Ivonne Delaflor embodies the enthusiasm and freedom of a child, coupled with the consciousness of a sincere spiritual seeker. This book contains a colorful feast of experiences that invite seekers to trust their hearts and divine grace in day-today life. The author describes with direct honesty her own challenges as a Westerner in India, transforming them into pure light. She responds to each situation with awareness, love, and compassion. There is joy and gratitude every step of the way. Ivonne's flowing style and humor make *India: The Journey of a Lifetime* a pleasure to read.

~ Linda Saccoccio (artist, Yoga instructor)
www.lindasaccoccio.com

*India: The Journey of a Lifetime* delivered in me a state of bliss and deep meditation. As a meditator for over 50 years now, the enjoyable reading and child-like energy of this book reminded me of the celebration and constant manifestation of the Divine in all forms. It is palpable the transmission, or Shaktipat, in the words written, which carries you through its story as a boat would carry you on the sea. Read, listen, and be attentive for as you read, *India: The Journey of a Lifetime* will invite your consciousness to receive the message beyond the message and the blessing of Prema, Divine Love.

~ Swamy Brahmanandapuri

# India

# India

✦

## The Journey of a Lifetime

*A Mystical, Magical Adventure That Opens the
Heart along the Way*

*Ivonne Delaflor
Foreword by Alex Slucki,
Author of **The Game of
Remembrance***

iUniverse, Inc.
New York  Lincoln  Shanghai

# India
## The Journey of a Lifetime

Copyright © 2005 by ivonne delaflor

iUniverse books may be ordered through booksellers or by contacting:

iUniverse
2021 Pine Lake Road, Suite 100
Lincoln, NE 68512
www.iuniverse.com
1-800-Authors (1-800-288-4677)

ISBN: 0-595-33856-9 (pbk)
ISBN: 0-595-67020-2 (cloth)

Printed in the United States of America

Dedicated as a humble offering
to all those with the focus on God's realization.
To sacred Mother India and all survivors of the Tsunami.
To Jovi, Alhia & Christian,
and to Sri Babaji Nagaraj, for the adventure that has just begun.

# *Contents*

Foreword . . . . . . . . . . . . . . . . . . . . . . . . . . . . . . . . . . . . . . . xiii

Introduction . . . . . . . . . . . . . . . . . . . . . . . . . . . . . . . . . . . . xvii

**CHAPTER 1**    A Portal Called India . . . . . . . . . . . . . . . . . . . 1

    Almost Ready . . . . . . . . . . . . . . . . . . . . . . . . . . . . . . . . 2

    Breaking through Fear . . . . . . . . . . . . . . . . . . . . . . . . . . 4

    Frankfurt . . . . . . . . . . . . . . . . . . . . . . . . . . . . . . . . . . . 6

    The Initiation . . . . . . . . . . . . . . . . . . . . . . . . . . . . . . . . 8

    The Portal Opens . . . . . . . . . . . . . . . . . . . . . . . . . . . . . 11

    On Being a Swamini . . . . . . . . . . . . . . . . . . . . . . . . . . . 13

    Pranams to Shiva . . . . . . . . . . . . . . . . . . . . . . . . . . . . . 15

    Sri Ramakrishna Math . . . . . . . . . . . . . . . . . . . . . . . . . 18

    Sri Sarada Devi . . . . . . . . . . . . . . . . . . . . . . . . . . . . . . 19

    Swami Vivekananda . . . . . . . . . . . . . . . . . . . . . . . . . . . 20

    Swami Premananda . . . . . . . . . . . . . . . . . . . . . . . . . . . 22

    The Mysterious Appointment . . . . . . . . . . . . . . . . . . . . 23

    The Divine Message . . . . . . . . . . . . . . . . . . . . . . . . . . . 26

    Siddha Yogi Sivashankar Baba . . . . . . . . . . . . . . . . . . . . 28

    The Puja . . . . . . . . . . . . . . . . . . . . . . . . . . . . . . . . . . . 32

    The Sacred Family . . . . . . . . . . . . . . . . . . . . . . . . . . . . 33

**CHAPTER 2**    The Divine Mother . . . . . . . . . . . . . . . . . . . . . . 36

    The Mother's Magical Embrace . . . . . . . . . . . . . . . . . . . 37

    The Positive Child Called Amma . . . . . . . . . . . . . . . . . . 40

    Questions to the Mother . . . . . . . . . . . . . . . . . . . . . . . . 42

    Nectar from the Gods . . . . . . . . . . . . . . . . . . . . . . . . . . 47

Brahmachari Dayamrita. . . . . . . . . . . . . . . . . . . . . . . . . . . . 48
Darshan. . . . . . . . . . . . . . . . . . . . . . . . . . . . . . . . . . . . . . . 51
To Cochin. . . . . . . . . . . . . . . . . . . . . . . . . . . . . . . . . . . . . 54
Embracing the World . . . . . . . . . . . . . . . . . . . . . . . . . . . . 56
The Convergence of Waters. . . . . . . . . . . . . . . . . . . . . . . . 61
Happy Birthday! . . . . . . . . . . . . . . . . . . . . . . . . . . . . . . . . 66

**CHAPTER 3    Masculine Energy. . . . . . . . . . . . . . . . . . . 69**
The Magic of Bangalore. . . . . . . . . . . . . . . . . . . . . . . . . . 70
The ISKON Temple . . . . . . . . . . . . . . . . . . . . . . . . . . . . . 74
Om Sri Sai Ram. . . . . . . . . . . . . . . . . . . . . . . . . . . . . . . . 76
Guru Brahma Story . . . . . . . . . . . . . . . . . . . . . . . . . . . . . 83
To Bangalore. . . . . . . . . . . . . . . . . . . . . . . . . . . . . . . . . . 87
New Delhi. . . . . . . . . . . . . . . . . . . . . . . . . . . . . . . . . . . . 90
Divine Love Story . . . . . . . . . . . . . . . . . . . . . . . . . . . . . . 91
The Taj Mahal. . . . . . . . . . . . . . . . . . . . . . . . . . . . . . . . . 95
Mathura. . . . . . . . . . . . . . . . . . . . . . . . . . . . . . . . . . . . . 100
Sri Aurobindo's Ashram. . . . . . . . . . . . . . . . . . . . . . . . . 103
Mr. J. Joseph . . . . . . . . . . . . . . . . . . . . . . . . . . . . . . . . . 106
A Lesson of Trust. . . . . . . . . . . . . . . . . . . . . . . . . . . . . . 108
Swami Nityananda. . . . . . . . . . . . . . . . . . . . . . . . . . . . . 110

**CHAPTER 4    Babaji Nagaraj, the Sacred Feet Experience . . . . . . 114**
Rishikesh and the Mystery of Babaji . . . . . . . . . . . . . . . . 115
Who is Babaji?. . . . . . . . . . . . . . . . . . . . . . . . . . . . . . . . 123

**CHAPTER 5    The Cherry on the Cake. . . . . . . . . . . . . . . . . 127**
Until Next Time . . . . . . . . . . . . . . . . . . . . . . . . . . . . . . 128
One year later . . . . . . . . . . . . . . . . . . . . . . . . . . . . . . . . 135

About the Author . . . . . . . . . . . . . . . . . . . . . . . . . . . . . . 139
Glossary of Sanskrit Terms . . . . . . . . . . . . . . . . . . . . . . . 141
Contact Information . . . . . . . . . . . . . . . . . . . . . . . . . . . . 145

# *Acknowledgments*

I feel most grateful to the President of India, A. P. J. Abdul Kalam, and his interest in sharing tools that can assist parents and children to evolve in spiritually balanced ways. Thank you. You were the trigger of a wonderful experience.

Akshmil, Devananda, Bhakti, and Govinda, thank you for such an unforgettable experience.

Prema Baba, thank you for the chosen silence and the wine of wisdom, and especially for the reconnection to Sri Babaji.

To my friend Alan S., thank you for the *rasamani* gift and for your generosity. You are a true friend. What else can I say?

Mr. J. Joseph, thank you for your refined and spiritual service.

Gautam, you truly are what your name represents—an enlightened one, an angel who inspired us to serve more without expecting anything from it. Thank you, dear friend.

Amma, thank you for hugging the spirit of your children with your soul.

Sai Baba, what a lesson! Thank you for welcoming us into your home.

Shankar Baba, not only are you a great teacher, but also you are fun! Thank you for the puja, for the blessings, and for all you do.

Swami Nityananda, what an inspiration of simplicity you are! Your presence removed my data regarding selfish gurus. (A projection of mine perhaps?) Thank you so much.

Mariela, you are an angel. Thank you for taking such good care of my little *gooroos*. And for having the heart-eyes to see Christian in its special-ness and uniqueness. May God bless you and your family forever.

Alan Cohen, thank you for the workshop you gave us in which I expressed my wish to go to India. You are a *true* teacher from the heart. Thank you.

Chick, thank you for the Parent Talk System, which was the first reason I was invited to India. Although we did not give any workshops, we did practice the language.

Claus, I love you. I felt your thoughts and your good wishes for my journey. Your trust in me humbles me more each day.

Universal Healer, thank you for the hero. You were right, it was very important for me to go to India.

Bhavani, you are a true demonstration of discipline, honesty, wisdom, and love!

Father, thank you for cheering me on to go to India. Thank you for being who you are.

Noefo, Om. Thank you for the work you did with the pictures on this book.

Rabia, thanks for keeping up with me and my writing and for doing such a focused and great job in such a short period of time! You are an angel!

Cris and Alex Almeida, you are a treasure of friendship.

Cynthia, Karla, Patricia, thank you for your love, kind words, and cheers regarding my trip to India and all I do.

Linda, Maggie, Swamy Brahmanandapuri, Br. Dayamrita, Swami Chetanananda, and Swami Ramananda, I feel deeply touched by the endorsements from the heart you wrote. Thank you.

Parvati, thank you for serving as the voice of Sri Babaji. All praise to his lotus feet.

Enrique, I love you. Thank you for all that has evolved, for your support to manifest India as a reality, and for doing the best you can. May you find God within.

God…Soulmate…Beloved of all times, to you I offer all my gratitude; for the experience of India, for the experience of love, and for your presence in my soul, which is the greatest adventure of my life.

# *Foreword*

Life is ten percent what happens to you
and ninety percent how you respond to it.
~ *Lou Holtz*

ABOUT TRUSTING GOD, RECOVERING THE MEMORY OF THE SACRED,
AND BEING HOME

Why I was so afraid to visit India is still a puzzling question. Perhaps it was due to all the programming received from different people, data that was far from the actual experience and the most exquisite truth. For the truth is, the moment we stepped down from the plane, my mind could only produce the sentence, *"I'm home."* We hadn't even seen the extraordinary sights of southern India: lush and colorful, watery and smooth like the river's surface.

I had been told there was a *"smell"* in India, but all I found was a fragrance. From the very beginning, this scent seemed to come from the eyes and soul of India's people. It was spicy like the food and yet sweet like the gazes of those who greeted us, always in the consciousness of service's sacredness, as Krishna would have it, "not thinking about the results, but the love of service itself." Were it from the airport to the next hotel, or from the hotel, or even an ashram, to our next destination, a sense of utter protection surrounded us by our guides and drivers. Yes, indeed it seemed we'd have to trust God upon seeing particular driving manners, but this seemed a necessary practice of tolerance, which led to our visiting incredible places.

In Madras, Angena led our journey. She introduced us to many of the deities—Ganesha, Shiva's son, and Durga and Hanuman, all of whom had many stories to tell. We also met Parvati, who was turned into a peacock for a lack of reverence to her husband, Shiva. Regardless of the nature of the stories, the deities always seemed to be playing the game of living, each representing various qualities: vigor, intelligence, sensibility, abundance, protection—all revered as aspects of the Self.

We also met two masters in Madras. Swamigal lived in a very humble home in the midst of alleyways and people. The other, Shankar Baba, had a very elegant approach to living and a wise humor that reminded us not to follow gurus blindly or to worry about our path, which, as he seemed to perceive, was unfolding precisely the way it should. He told us to trust God or the gods. He had family albums, pictures of Krishna, Hanuman, and Agni manifesting as fire during a [1]puja ceremony or in midst of meditation. He spoke of them as he would of cousins and brothers, friends and associates. I couldn't help but think they actually were his family. Was he saying to us that all is one, and we are all the same?

Cochin brought Amma and an awakening consciousness to service. How could words describe the power of a human who could embrace the whole of humanity? The eyes of compassion itself, *"the transmission of Shakti with a single hug,"* where surrender and a little piece of heaven are available. Amma was certainly a reminder that there is always energy to offer love and service to Source. We saw her repeatedly, in her beautiful ashram, in the little fishermen's village, and once more in the huge stadium.

Same woman, same attitude, same reverence from others toward that which she represents: the Mother, the presence of true, unconditional love. How far can our soul reach in terms of touching others? How much can we give? These are questions that continue to ripple inside me, like the stone cast from our journey to India.

Puttaparthi brought Sai Baba's magnificence into play. We had heard so much of Sai Baba. He has been deified by many, turned into a god by the people who surround him. Is he God or is he a man? Can miracles be used as a means to differentiate the common man from the saint? Did not Christ say that all men could perform these miracles, especially the miracle of love? Aren't we recipients, each and every human, of this same essence, the liquid of existence itself? Oh, Sai Baba, my own higher self was claiming to decree in your presence, "You and I are always and have always been one." Sai Baba has created a city of delight—music, books, museum, temples, and a hospital. What is the meaning of sainthood? When will we consider these the efforts of a truly loving spirit and a very sacred man, just any man? When will models become a common reality on this planet? Those are the questions my visit to Sai Baba brought to my heart and mind.

---

1.    * "Pu" means "pushpam" or flower and "ja" means "jal" or water. In the puja ceremony both flowers and water are offered to the deity during the worship. The letter "ja" can also mean simultaneously "japam." So if we take these twin meanings of "ja" into consideration, puja becomes that ceremony during which water and flowers are offered to God along with recitation of His names In Hinduism puja is the most popular form of divine worship. As described in http://www.hinduwebsite. com/symbolisminpuja.htm

We visited Agra, Mathura, and Bangalore. We visited Delhi, the capital of India. Like branches of a tree, we stretched all the way to Rishikesh. There were so many signs that told us to go there to meet the unmeetable Babaji. A journey unexpected, like the sudden leaves of these many branches giving fruit never before tasted. We were filled with the presence of the gurus at the Kriya Yoga center. We met Nityananda, the grounding soul, the child-like one, filled with basic wisdom, the power of simplicity.

The thread that wove all of this together, like the beads of a beautiful necklace, a symbol of beauty and refinement—my sister, Ivonne, *Swamini Amenanda*, a beautiful warm, engaging, loving and real young mystic. She, drunken in God's presence in everything and everyone, astonished me when she ate, when she greeted the plants, when she thanked existence over and over for such a memorable creation. She, who helped me catalyze my own self in order to remember that there is always more celebration—more and more and more. Her enthusiasm is infectious, and she adequately transports us in this book not only to new places and culture but also to the heart of spirituality and oneness.

As you read *INDIA; The Journey of a Lifetime*, you will feel a subtle spiritual transformation and a refined sense of appreciation for India and Ivonne's magical journey, which reminds us to dance and enjoy every moment as the one and only moment, rebirthing the awareness that we are the creators of endless possibilities of magic and love in this journey called life.

For one must dance in the circle, participating in the exuberance of life. One must be in the ritual and must sleep less in order to celebrate more. One must do *nothing* in particular, for choices are always part of the game. I choose here and now, thanks to myself and this journey, thanks to my beautiful companions, to India and its people, to the many gurus, to pulse in the bliss of existence—to love and serve—to be aware. To breathe, to breathe the presence of Amenai in, like a wind of sacredness in order to reach the highest experience and share it with fellow beings.

All my love to you all,
Alex Slucki,
Swami Akshmilananda Giri
Author of *The Game of Remembrance*
www.huellasdeluz.com

# Introduction

Own only what you can carry with you;
Know language, know countries, and know people.
Let your memory be your travel bag.
~ *Alexander Solzhenitsyn*

In early 2003, I was participating in a workshop with Mr. Alan Cohen. He gave us an assignment to write the ten things that first come to mind with the statement, "If I were not afraid, I would..."

The first thing that came to my mind was, "I would go to India." The thought caught me by surprise, but it was only an answer in an exercise.

A few months later, a message I received through the Internet piqued my attention. It came from the private secretary of the President of India sharing their interest in what I was doing in Mexico: "The Parent Talk Workshops," and my "working" book, *The Positive Child*. They were intrigued about the concept of empowering the positive mind in children through the language of love. They told me they were very interested in my workshops and told me to contact the [1]Mata Amritananda Mayi Math Ammachi Organization, which would receive a call from the president's office letting them know about me.

A few weeks later I received an e-mail from a person named Gautam, living in India. (I never imagined he was going to be a major key of possibilities, consciousness, and demonstration of unconditional love for me). At that time, I was in the WOW state.

From a very early age, I had felt a deep connection to India—its food, practices, and customs. When I was twelve years old, I wanted to know more about India. My interest in meditation arose in my heart at that time. I also became a

---

1.  A spiritual organization with innumerable humanitarian activities all over the world. Some of them are free food and clothing programs, charitable hospitals, hospices, disaster relief programs, free homes for the poor and the needy, medical camps, orphanages, schools, educational institutions, widows' pension scheme, free legal advice, preservation of nature, and so on. Data extracted from http://ammachi.org/humanitarian-activities/index.html

vegetarian, first relinquishing meat, then chicken, then fish, and then, *Viva la vida veggie!*

Anyway, when I first read Gautam's message, his name moved something in me. The life of [2]Siddhartha Gautama Buddha had been my introduction to the experience of consciousness, service, compassion, and how not to be judgmental. I took this as a sign from the Divine and joyfully read Gautam's messages. I told him about what the President of India wanted me to share and the interest I had in sharing it with Ammachi's community. Then he told me that they wanted to send me an invitation to the *50th birthday celebration of Amma*. The theme, *EMBRACING THE WORLD*, went as a shiver from the top of my head to the bottom of my feet. Until that moment, I thought Ammachi's group was a traditional school or a business—anything except what I was about to discover.

Without a second thought, I said *yes* to the invitation. Later, I began thinking about all the arrangements and details necessary in order to embark on this crazy adventure. I have two beautiful little *goo-roos*—my children—who needed proper conscious attention and loving care if I were going to go to India.

A couple of weeks passed. Upon returning home one day, I saw a beautiful, impeccable, well-presented, professional envelope—the invitation for Amma's birthday celebration. It was to be held at Cochin Kerala from September 23 to 28, 2003. It also included an invitation to stay at her ashram.

That afternoon, I took my children to one of their activities in a place called Mundo Pequeño. The coordinator of [3]*Mastery Life A.C.* is the owner there and a very dear friend in consciousness to me. I told her that I was going to India and her reply was, "Me too!" Friends and acquaintances of mine began hearing that I was going, and then six of the members of *Mastery Life* A.C. agreed to join me on an unexpected India adventure. I had taken a big leap of faith toward the unknown, supported by many of my friends!

---

2.    Buddha was born approximately 560 B.C. in the land of Northern India. Through his life, Buddha gave the concept of Nirvana an unprecedented exposure to a large portion of the Eastern world with his achievement of and subsequent teachings about the state of enlightenment. As a religion, Buddhism contains the attainment of Buddhahood or Nirvana as a central tenet of its teachings. Data extracted from http://www.cosmicharmony.com/Av/Buddha/Buddha.htm

3.    A spiritual-conscious organization that aims to empower the development of conscious living in the here and now through information on self-development, spirituality, health, healing, and other related subjects. Ivonne Delaflor serves as founder of the organization since the year 2002. www.masterylife.com

Months and details evolved, along with our activities in Cancun, but our main priority still was our families and children. We researched the best prices of hotels, airline tickets, and so on. But the missing piece for us all was the conscious care of our children while we were away. We kept our focus on *trusting* the process. After many weeks of intense search, my dear husband and a beautiful, kind and patient nanny agreed to stay with my children. The rest of my friends also successfully resolved their childcare issues as well. Now it was time to manifest the trip!

The details began to fall into place as quickly as a refreshing summer rain, smoothly, and magically! One day I e-mailed a friend, Mrs. Delia Amezquita, letting her know I was going to India. She immediately told me that her teacher also would be there at exactly the same time. She said, "It would be very nice if you can meet him. He will be guiding the [4]Navaratri, and his name is Swami Nityananda."

My heart and mind smiled. I used to have a teacher, a disciple of Swami Muktananda's and a very good friend of Swami Nityananda, who was chosen to continue Swami Muktananda's work and his *Shakti* (Divine Energy), which was very strong. The leela (play of consciousness) was already playing with me, and my heart just said yes, I would meet with Swami Nityananda.

I was about to let her know my decision to meet Nityananda, when a little advertising box popped up on my computer screen and, amazingly, the ad was for a travel agency in India! Without knowing anything about them but trusting that this was an agency managed by God, I sent them my interest in a pilgrimage to India and told them the dates and possible places I wanted to go.

That night my friends Bhaktiananda, Devananda, Govinda, and Akshmilan-daji gathered in my home to have our weekly meditation and to discuss the manifestation of our India trip. We agreed that the focus was our transformation. We needed to keep the awareness that there was truly no place to go—whether we traveled to India, Siberia, Paris, or nowhere, our focus was on evolution and con-

---

4.  A popular festival celebrated in India, and one of the longest. Like the other festivals of India, Navaratri is rich in meaning. At one level, Navaratri signifies the progress of a spiritual aspirant. During this spiritual journey, the aspirant has to pass three stages personified by Durga, Lakshmi, and Saraswati. Then, he or she enters into the realm of the infinite, wherein one realizes one's Self. Navaratri, which literally means "nine nights," dedicates three days each to worshipping the Divine in the forms of Durga, Lakshmi, and Saraswati. The tenth day, though, is the most important; it is known as Vijayadashami, the "tenth day of victory." http://www.amritapuri. org/cultural/bharat/navaratri.htm

sciousness. We were still in Cancun and that was exactly where we needed to be. When we would be in India, we would be in India. Otherwise our bodies could be in Cancun, and our heads would be in India, and the focus might get a little unbalanced.

We also agreed that I would prepare the itinerary—the places we should visit, the hotels we would stay in, and so on. Then I told my friends I had found an agency about which I knew nothing but that my heart felt was right. (Although I must confess to a little doubt. It was just a "noise," having had the experience that sometimes people tend to abuse or take advantage of people who trust. My heart was more powerful than that "noise," so I followed it once again!). I prayed to God that all our creation was based in pure intention, celebration, and love and thanked Him for my friends' trust of me in this endeavor.

It was right to trust. The Indian travel agency sent me one of their angels, Mr. J. Joseph, who was not only 100 percent professional, but also a very loving and spiritual man. He maintained his gratitude and excellent service through the entire two-month period of choices and decisions and periods of waiting time due to the time difference between Mexico and India.

I continue corresponding everyday with Mr. J. Joseph through the Internet, and by September 13, our tour was beautifully prepared and we were ready to go. On September 17, the Super Five would meet at Miami International Airport to start a journey that would change our lives forever.

Now, close your eyes for a moment before starting to read this real life adventure. Invite your mind to remain quiet from judgments and expectations through the journey you will take along with us. Breathe deeply and smile, which will balance both your brain hemispheres and will relinquish any seriousness you have and bring a sense of relief.

Inside of me, India will live forever. I don't remove the possibility in my mind of going back. I love adventures and meeting new people. I also feel deep gratitude for that sacred land.

I did not go to India to find the meaning of life. I was not looking for the cave to enlightenment. I did not go to find a guru or want to be a renunciate. I went to India because my heart desired it. The invitation to go came in the most magical way; everything evolves to support our unfolding adventure. I went to India for the adventure and with the trust that everything manifests in the Divine order and God's plan—even the things I don't particularly like sometimes. My trip to India also represented an opportunity for me to really *be* with myself, which I hadn't done at all since I had my first child five-and-a-half years ago.

With the non-expectations and the imminent trust that was needed for this type of adventure, my traveling companions and I met wonderful human beings who had realized God within themselves. We met extraordinary healers and guides. We visited magnificently blessed temples. We experienced silence, contemplation, and meditation in magical and fun ways. I feel blessed for having had the experiences, for having met such wonderful beings, and for encountering four wonderful gurus: my dear friends who came along for the adventure. India's resemblance to Mexico—its mysticism, prayers, and the innocence of its people, will live always in my soul.

We don't need to travel far for a grand adventure, for the moment, this moment—the one and only moment—is the greatest adventure of all. This is currently my prayer and what makes this book unique by reminding us that life is a totally magical experience! As Prema Baba Swamiji once said, "There is nowhere to go. All the nectar you need is right here where you are."

I wish God's realization and everlasting love for all children of planet Earth and for all of us.

I ask you to take a deep breath and to open your heart to join me in this journey.

AND NOW:

GET READY,

SET,

OM!!!!

And to *India* we go to experience *The Journey of a Lifetime*!

Ivonne Delaflor, the author, is also known as Swami Amenanda or
Amenai as her close friends call her. © Mastery Life A.C

# 1

## *A Portal Called India*

In your womb humanity arises,
Oh, sweet land of the mystics
You give whispers of hope to many
While your colors transpire the divine form of creation.

Oh, Lord Shiva, Oh, Brahma, Oh, Krishna…
In your land the destiny is being written,
And thy people are the kindred spirits of the new world.

You will resurrect from the ashes like the phoenix;
Your eyes will speak to the world of Love.
May all beings be bathed in your wisdom…
Oh, sweet INDIA; my heart Pranams to you.

*~ Ivonne Delaflor*

# Almost Ready

*Love is the way messengers from the Mystery tell us things.*
*~ Rumi*

Two days before traveling to India, the awareness that I was actually going there hit me strongly. I suddenly realized *I am going to India!* A deep, internal flood of emotions and thoughts took life in my mind. All the stories I'd heard, the fact that I would leave my children for more than five days for the very first time, the unknown aspects of traveling, illnesses, diseases, impressions—many, many thoughts ran through my mind. Programming data, manifestations, and attachments to ideas and concepts began arising. Honestly, I was beginning to experience panic as my heart raced and my legs trembled softly. Although it was a well-controlled panic, it was panic nonetheless. Statements such as, "This is happening," or "It is all for the best," began to be affirmations regarding my adventurous nature to follow my heart, my instincts, and my dreams. My nights were mostly sleepless with the excitement and the recognition of the new doorway of possibilities I had just opened—what was going to be, and what was already being, a most transcendental journey. My mind was clearing out all the attachments in order to enjoy what would be one of the most magical journeys of my life!

The last forty-eight hours were spent preparing myself and making sure I left everything in proper order for my children. I was pretty relaxed in this regard since my husband and a wonderful "nangel," Mariela (Yes, "nan" for nanny and "gel" for angel!), were going to be in charge of my little goo-roos.

Packing and unpacking consumed my time. I created a huge list of things for us to take based on suggestions of people living in India and the advice of Westerners who thought the situation in India was always hazardous for anyone's health.

From baby wipes to organic bathroom cleaners, from towels to candles, from multivitamins to Chinese remedies for Montezuma's Revenge, and, of course, healthy protein bars and water-purifying drops. My very well-prepared suitcase was as heavy as my two children put together. I also included a book by [1]Prema Baba Swamiji, [2]*The Initiation*, a notebook, camera, clothes, and a white shawl.

---

1.    Prema Baba Swamiji (Respected Father of Higher Love). Co-Founder with Swami Leelananda of The Modern Order of Swamis and The Power of Love Foundation. www.spiritualjava.com
    Author of the book *The Initiation*. http://www.spiritualjava.com/about.php.

In India, the right hand is used for eating while the left hand is used for "unclean" duties. Due to a car accident and my near-death experience exactly thirteen years ago, the mobility of my right arm, especially my right hand is impaired. Although I have found new ways of moving it, I've been eating with my left hand all these years. So, in addition to all the other supplies, I also had to pack a special armband that I often use when my right hand is tired. Until then, I was not aware that I still had issues regarding this challenge. Facing it again was a major breakthrough for me.

---

2.    The Initiation is a journey of self-discovery, allowing abundant possibilities. With the power to open minds, Swamiji's words allow a spiritual awakening, and an affirmation of identity. A true story capturing one man's profound experience in India, The Initiation bears a timeless, transformational message. www.amazon.com

# Breaking through Fear

From craving is born grief,
from craving is born fear.
For one freed from craving
there's no grief
—so why fear?
~ DHAMMAPADA, verse 216,
*translated by Thanissaro Bhikkhu*

Wednesday, September 17, was the first time in my married life that I was ready without being rushed by my husband. Ready even earlier than expected, I felt like a child who is used to her parents' assistance and this was my very first time traveling. I felt ready for an evolving adventure!

Saying farewell to my children was the most difficult part of leaving. I couldn't stop thinking of [3] *The Bhagavad-Gita* in which Krishna requests Arjuna to detach from everything he knows and trust completely in the Lord. That was what I was doing. At the airport, with tears in my eyes, I said farewell to my beautiful gooroos, my husband, and Nangel. By the time I arrived at the gate, I felt like a teenager—excited and ready for a great adventure. I felt like dancing, fearless, and the freshness of adventuring into the unknown. My seat number was nine and along with the number five and number eleven, these numbers accompanied me through my entire journey.

When we took off (my seat number was eighty-one—the number nine again, if you add them), I was determined to sleep. But during the next eight hours, I encountered someone I was not expecting: *My self.* I was alone for the first time in months. No one sat in the seat beside me, and many empty spaces surrounded me. I was with myself—a journey from recognition of my unconsciousness to my personal power. Moments of tears, smiles, and the wanting to stop my mind once and for all. Eight hours with myself without being able to avoid it!

I could feel as if a deep ancient ritual was being lived inside my being. I felt a deep cleansing of memories and went through different stages of the mind; from breakthroughs through illuminated moments, I felt I was experiencing a sacred

---

3.    Considered to be the most sacred and popular scripture of Hinduism. It is the discourse of God which is revealed to us through the conversation between Him and Arjuna in the battlefield of Kurukshetra. It deals with the secrets of undertaking our responsibilities with a sense of detachment and keeping calm amidst the humdrum of daily mundane life. http://www.hinduwebsite.com/gitaindex.htm

Initiation unto the ever open door to the Divine. So much work remained to do within myself! Guilt emerged along with thoughts regarding unconscious moments with my loved ones over the past few months. Remorse and repentance came next, and then prayers requesting new opportunities. Gratitude also was present toward all experiences in my life. I was living a birth and rebirth on a plane!

Three days before I began traveling, I requested my astrological aspects from Carolina, my longtime friend, astrology teacher, and a beautiful being I had been honored to know for almost ten years. She e-mailed me the aspects of my traveling when she consulted her astrological charts with the dates I gave her. What she told me in short was: "It is a birth and rebirth experience. Amazing things will happen. Magic, magic, and more magic."

I took three deep breaths, gave thanks to existence for the experience of being human, closed my eyes, and let go in to a short resting time with only one thought in mind: *How blessed I felt to be alive!*

# Frankfurt

*No matter how bad a state of mind you may get into,*
*If you keep strong and hold out, eventually the floating clouds*
*Must vanish and the withering wind must cease.*
*~ Dogen*

In Frankfurt we had a layover of approximately five hours, and we decided to venture a walk and a visit to the city. We didn't get that far. A walk outside the airport to stretch and smell the "pure air" was all we could manage. Odd—everywhere we saw people smoking. The rancid and dense smell of the smoke was overwhelming and, after only forty-five minutes, we returned to the airport.

We drank some tea and hot chocolate, and then they announced that our flight was ready to board. In the waiting area, the view began to have an Indian flavor. Women with their beautiful [4]saris, the amazing dance they do with their heads, people with a red dot between the brows painted in red, and their beautiful smiles. What a nice view! I began to "smell" my Hindu data popping up.

Then the time came to hand over our boarding passes, but suddenly mine was missing! A few minutes before that, my dear friend Alex, Swami Akshmilanandaji, was doing my [5]Mayan astrology, telling me that I should be more attentive to details and focused on order. My inattention and distraction had quickly manifested. I took a deep breath and frantically began searching for my boarding pass. I thought, "There is a lesson here to learn." Then I began feeling the appropriateness of the moment.

I was ready to take out my credit card to buy another ticket, but a very tall man, dressed in a white shirt, with soft black hair, a gentle voice, and a sweet smile told me to look for it carefully in my bag. That same man with a big smile said, "You are the second person I was able to help today!" I was so grateful, not only for not having to spend additional money, but for the lesson and demonstration of service. I was honored to meet someone like him. What a beautiful way God let me know that everything is being taken care of, always by Source! The incident also made me more careful and attentive to the moment.

Again we boarded, and again my seat was eighty-one. Again I was alone. This time I slept and then watched a movie, *Bruce Almighty.* My mind, my imagina-

---

4.    Sari is an unstitched and uncut, rectangular piece of cloth worn by women in the Indian sub-continent. http://www.puja.com/sari/whtsr/whtsr.htm

5.    The Mayan Astrology is a system based in the Mayan calendar and is all about cycles that are considered the weave of creation. http://www.mayanmajix.com

tion, and my inner chills took this as a powerful sign from God. Everything was just too perfect! It always is! The messages, the signs, God, God, and more God everywhere I looked.

My stomach was becoming a huge temple of butterflies as the time got closer for our arrival in India. I started meditating and praying and then took out the books I had with me, *The Initiation*.

# The Initiation

This is it. This is the moment.
The glory and love of God is here in this moment.
Heaven is in this moment.
Enlightenment is in this very moment. This is it!
If we don't learn here and now to appreciate it, what will ever satisfy us?
~ *Prema Baba Swamiji*
*(Excerpt from The Initiation)*

Dr. Donald Schnell, or as his disciples lovingly call him, Baba, wrote a beautiful book about his extraordinary experience in India meeting Mahavatar Babaji, the famous immortal living Master of the Himalayas. In November of 1997, he was led to a remote temple in India where he was initiated by [6]*Babaji*, receiving *The New Spirituality* his blessing of prema, "Divine Love," and was asked by Babaji to bring his blessings to the West.

Swami Paramahansa Yogananda first described Babaji in his book, *Autobiography of a Yogi*, as the ever-living master of all ages. Prema Baba Swamiji shares his experience in *The Initiation*, which transmits his Shakti subtly and powerfully. The words are written in a melodious way, making the experience seem like a metaphysical story. A wonderful transmission of love from a human being like you and me, *The Initiation* is an open invitation for all to love and experience prema and share it with everyone.

For some time, I had been having dreams and experiencing a longing to find a teacher, even though I already had a meditation teacher. My personal life was undergoing a major transformation, from limited beliefs, difficult situations in my marriage, and an unknown and deep spiritual longing, and I was having intense moments as my spiritual thirst grew stronger. Shortly afterward, I had the honor of meeting Dr. Schnell and his wife, whom I invited to Cancun. Upon meeting him, I felt deep emotion and celebration. We exchanged the real blessing of the energy in the recognition of oneness and love. Before our meeting, Baba's wife sent me the book. I began reading it while sitting on the deck of a boat in the middle of the ocean in Cancun. A heavy sleepiness embraced my being and, as I was closing my eyes, I saw Mahavatar Babaji's form in the sky inside of a huge tri-

---

6.    The deathless **Babaji** is an Avatar who had retained His physical form for centuries.
www.ascension-research.org

angle. I opened my eyes and found my breathing was exalted and the longing to meet Babaji was very profound.

Many things evolved from that moment on. My relationship with the meditation teacher I had for five years came to completion. And the transmission of Babaji was present at all times through the energy of Prema Baba. It took me some time, though, to realize the magic of it.

Baba and his wife stayed in Cancun for a month and shared their wisdom through selfless service and numerous workshops. We went on a magical journey to a sacred [7]Temazcal with friends. We also traveled to [8]Chichen-Itza *during* the full moon, guided by the recognized and respected Mexican archeologist and spiritual teacher of the Mayan (Itzae) culture, Adalberto Rivera. He is the archeologist who discovered the Serpent descending during the Equinox at Chichen, the incredible phenomenon that happens on two unique days of the year, March 21 and September 22, in the Kukulcan Pyramid built by the Mayans in honor of Kukulcan, the feathered serpent. The equinoxes create the illusion of his descent to join his worshippers. That night we experienced the magic of the pyramids, the sacred and ancient ritual of the Mayan Initiation to higher spirituality, where only those ready to relinquish the ego and offer their heart to a life of selfless service and love were honored with the blessings of wisdom. We felt the solitude and magnificence of the temples, we heard flutes playing, ancient ones, the stars shined as bright as the radiant sun, and the presence of God and the magic of Mahavatar Babaji was felt by all of us who felt gifted to experience such a unique and once-in-a-lifetime experience.

Since then, Prema Baba became a strong connection to India for me, and his presence in my life turned out to be a deep initiation. That connection allowed me to break the mental umbilical cords I had with "guru fantasies" but also

---

7.  A pre-Hispanic steam bath that was in general use in Mesoamerican cultures, the oldest vestiges of which can be found in the archeological zones of such as Palenque in Mexico and Piedras Negras in Guatemala. Its use throughout history has been ceremonial as well as therapeutic. The practice survives today thanks to the oral tradition of Mexican indigenous communities. The word Temazcal comes from the Nahuatl language and means steam house (temaz = steam, calli = house). http://www.go-oaxaca.com/tohil/what_is_temazcal_tohil.htm

8.  Chichén Itzá, the ancient city whose name means "in the mouth at the Itzáe's Well," was, in its time of grandeur between AD 800 and 1200, the center of political, religious, and military power in Yucatán, if not all of Southeastern Meso America. http://www.internet-at-ork.com/hos_mcgrane/chichen/chichen_index.html

invited me silently to grow, to share with others through workshops, and to truly believe in what I was doing.

Now, a year later, I remembered all of these connections while reading the introduction to the book while on the plane. How grateful I felt for having the opportunity to have met such wonderful beings in my life: Dr. Schnell, Adalberto, and all my friends in Cancun. I was blessed with the ability to see that all beings are the temples of my beloved Soulmate—my Soulmate called God.

I opened the book at random; on the page was Babaji's mantra gift to Prema Baba:

[9]OM

PURNAMADAH

*PURNAMIDAM*

*PURNAT PURNAMUDAACHYATE*

*PURNASYA PURNAMADAYA*

*PURNAMEVA VASHISYATE*

I began singing it over and over again with a deep intention of invoking Babaji's presence. The pilot announced that we were descending to Chennai. I closed the book—my spiritual guide. I closed my eyes and kissed the book, celebrating my courage to be there while the butterflies were flying stronger than ever inside my soul!

---

9.    The translation of this mantra is the sound of creation is sacred and holy. It births itself from the sacred and remains holy forever.

# The Portal Opens
## Madras, September 18

Help thy brother's boat across and thine own has reached the shore.
*~ Hindu proverb*

I had with me a little bag where I kept the orange shawl given to me by Prema Baba Swamiji, some sacred *malas* (also called prayer beads that are used by Hindus, Tibetans, and Yoga practitioners to count the repetitions of a mantra or of other sadhanas, spiritual practices) that my dearest friend Ana Quijano, (Taraji), gave me to use the moment I arrived in India, and a white shawl.

Weeks before my departure, Taraji came to my house with two beautiful malas. One was made out of ice crystal from the Tibetan Himalayas, the other of silver beads. She told me that I should wear the shawl covering my head and wear the malas before taking my first steps on the sacred soil of India. Then, upon my return, I should bring them back to her charged with all the energy of my experience there.

Taraji then told me the story of her silver mala. When she was visiting India many years ago, they went into a Tibetan temple. The monks there were waiting for a certain number of "right people" to walk into the temple. At a specific time, a bell would ring, and it just so happened that my dear friends Taraji and Luis walked through the door of the temple on the "right" day at the "right" time. The monks greeted them, giving them gifts. One of those was the silver mala I was about to wear. How honored I was that my friend thought of me to wear it and have it blessed by Mother India. With the white shawl on my head, my orange swamini shawl around my shoulders, and my mala around the neck, I was ready to take my first steps in Chennai, Madras.

We arrived at 11:55 PM and although the airport was old, a huge, beautiful painting from the *Bhagavad-Gita* that illustrated a scene where Krishna (one of the most commonly worshipped deities in the Hindu faith. He is considered to be the eight avatar of Lord Vishnu) is speaking to Arjuna (considered a great warrior and archer of the epic, the Mahabharata, and the initiator of the great preaching of Lord Krishna) was hanging on the wall. The message was: Focus not on the fruits of your work but on the work itself! All my friends were smiling with tears in their eyes, quiet from the long flight and from the reverberation of finally being in India. I was too excited in the moment, like a small child observing everything, to cry! I prayed to dear Mr. Joseph to have sent someone to pick us up. After passing through Customs, we picked up our suitcases and came out to the arrival room. A well-dressed man, wearing white, stood with a sign: Swamini Amenanda.

# On Being a Swamini

I am a little pencil in the hand of a writing God
Who is sending a love letter to the world.
~ *Mother Teresa*

The body is called a field, Arjuna; he who knows it is called the Knower of the
field. This is the knowledge of those who know.
I am the Knower of the field in everyone, Arjuna.
Knowledge of the field and its Knower is true knowledge.
~ Bhagavad-Gita *13:1–2*

When Prema Baba Swamiji was in Cancun in 2002, my dear sister-in-law and I
were invited to a special darshan (the grace-bestowing view of Divinity). Swami
Leelananda received us. The energy was strong in the room, and incense and candles were burning. After our arrival, Prema Baba entered the room and began a
beautiful ritual in which he was initiating us as [10]swaminis. My mind was in awe.
This was evidently nothing I had ever experienced before. He performed a grace-
ful, symbolic shaving of my head. The moment was sacred and beautiful. There
were no thoughts or emotions. My mind had just stopped. I watched Claudia
being initiated too, receiving her name with tears in her eyes and with respect and
honor.

It took me time to realize that being named as a swamini would have such
powerful impact in me, for the blessing and the transmission that happened that
day carried a powerful energy in a very subtle form. That day I did not see the gift
delivered into my heart. It was not just receiving a "Spiritual Title" in which,
honestly, I am far from interested. In time, however, I have discovered that being
ordained as a swamini is a powerful reminder to serve. To be a disciple and practitioner of love, to keep to my word, learn from my mistakes, to keep to my
word, and to have grand humbleness in whatever manifests in my life—these are
the responsibilities of that title.

---

10.    The word swami means master; it means striving for the mastery over one's smaller
self and habit patterns, so that the eternal Self within may come shining through.
The act of becoming a swami is not so much an acting of becoming, of adding on,
of allegiance, as it is an act of setting aside, of renunciation. A swami is one who has
set aside all of the limited, worldly pursuits, so as to devote full time effort to the
direct experience of the highest spiritual realization and to the service of others along
those lines. Data from http://www.swamij.com/what-is-a-swami.htm

I was named Swamini Amenanda (The Bliss of Truth); the word "Amen" means Truth or "so be it." Claudia, my sister in law, was given the name Ananda (Bliss). As my journey evolved in India, I discovered that the real swami lives in the heart. No robes, no renunciation, no extreme disciplines are necessary to serve, love, and assist others.

This beautiful memory was evolving in my mind and having just arrived in India, I felt like bowing and offering [11]*Namaste* to the person who came to pick us up in Chennai. Everything was more than perfect.

I must admit, however, that the driving in India was fast—a spiritual Disneyland for us. We traveled not only with luggage but also with *Trust!* There it was, another grand lesson. Our hotel was not far from the airport. The welcoming was nice, although the concierge was very surprised to receive young swamis—especially Western swamis who laughed out loud!

I shared a room with Leti (Letika), Devanandaji. She amazed me with her grand capacity to sleep. I felt really grateful to be with her. I barely slept two hours. I meditated during the night and was ready to go to meet beautiful India when the morning arrived.

Our breakfast buffet included Indian buffalo milk curd, chapattis,(delicious tortilla-type bread made with whole wheat flour, salt, oil, and softened butter), and paneer (a condensed type of fresh cottage cheese). Mmmhhh! Delicious! We drank wonderful masala tea, a delicious full-bodied, broken-leaf India black tea blended with ginger, cinnamon, and vanilla. Then we met our first spiritual tourist guide, Angena, a beautiful young Brahmin who spoke very clear English and French. She was sharp, practical, and elegant. We began our magical journey in her white Qualis (very much like a Toyota).

The first encounter we had with India was the amazing driving lessons you get for free! Yes, lessons based on sharp reflexes, excellent brakes, and total leaps of trust! The car and truck horns were like music; they are a communication system. In the West, people use their car horns to express anger or call attention to someone who is not moving fast enough. In India, horns are useful devices of survival communication!

Angena took us first to greet Lord Shiva.

---

11.   The gesture, Namaste, represents the belief there is a Divine spark within each of us that is located in the heart chakra. The gesture is an acknowledgment of the soul in one by the soul in another. *Nama* means "bow", *as* means "I", and *te* means "you." Therefore, Namaste literally means ""bow to me" or "I bow to you." http://www.yogajournal.com/practice/700.cfm

# Pranams to Shiva
## Kapaleeswarar Koil

The universe rises from you like bubbles rising from the sea.
Thus know the Self to be One and in this way
Enter into the state of dissolution.
~ *Astavakara Samhita*

The first construction of this Shiva temple was submerged under the sea. We visited the reconstruction of it. Deities from Annamalaiyar, Murugar, Saneeswara, Durgai, Dakshinamurthy, and Chandikeswarar are praised and worshiped here. Leaving our shoes and bags in the car, my Western-programmed mind was concerned that it wasn't safe enough. Our driver, a tall man, with big and deep beautiful brown eyes looked straight into my eyes with an "of course it is" look in his eyes. Here was one more opportunity for me to let go of programmed concepts.

We walked barefoot in the street; the temple was undergoing some remodeling. We bought beautiful jasmine garlands for ten rupees, (about twenty-five cents) that Bhakti, Devananda, and I wore around our heads. I also bought a lotus flower, and then we walked inside the temple. My heart was pumping strongly.

Angena began to tell us the story of the temple while serving as our bodyguard from all the vendors who wanted to sell us different pictures of the deities inside the temple, and jasmine and fragrant frangipani garlands to offer to the gods.

She explained the beautiful story of Shiva, Parvati, and Ganesha, in which it is said that one day Lord Shiva, while addressing Parvati, his wife, noticed that Parvati was not paying attention to him. She was tired of his delays when getting home and never letting her know about his plans, so she ignored him. That infuriated Shiva who, in his rage, turned Parvati into a peacock. The magic of the peacock represented Parvati, Shiva's Shakti. Then she proceeded sharing the story of Ganesha, who is the son of Shiva and Parvati. He is a beautiful, strong, and luminous child. One day Shiva goes to one of his battles and pilgrimages and, while he is away, his son grows without knowing what his father looks like. One day Shiva returns, and his son, Ganesha, opens the door when Shiva knocks, but because he doesn't recognize him, Ganesha doesn't allow Shiva to come in the house. Shiva, not recognizing his son, was furious and cut off his head! Parvati came along screaming and in tears saying, "What have you done to our son?" Shiva immediately saw an elephant passing by, cut its head as well, and placed it in the body of Ganesha. Parvati then was happy, and since then elephants are revered as sacred and so is Ganesha as the protector of homes and spiritual practices.

We were contemplating and visualizing the stories while we followed Angena, like little children, wherever she wanted to take us and listened to all her stories. I felt intoxicated with love. I was not at all experiencing what many other people had told me—India smelled bad, and the views were obscured by all the beggars. The jasmine flowers and the sandalwood incense filled the air with freshness and spiritual fragrance. Everyone was part of the beautiful mysticism of Mother India. I experienced the tangible compassion and trusted that everything was perfect with the universe.

Over lunch Angena said that she received a call the night after meeting us announcing that we had decided to use her services for the next two days. She was grateful due to lack of business at this time. Now she said she felt more grateful to be in the presence of a spiritually minded group that was teaching her so many things. We felt exactly the same way.

Then she shared another beautiful story about [12] *Kali,* one of the goddesses, where she is said to have emanated from the brow of Goddess Durga (slayer of demons) during one of the battles between the Divine and anti-Divine forces. Etymologically, Durga's name means "Beyond Reach." She is thus an echo of the woman warrior's fierce virginal autonomy. In this context Kali is considered the "forceful" form of the great goddess, Durga. Angena continued to tell us stories from Indian mythology and sacred scriptures while we were eating wonderful Indian food and beautifully prepared coconut desserts baked in spicy and tangy ginger and, of course, excellent masala tea that flavored our tongue not only with cardamom but also with ecstatic bliss.

After lunch, we hurriedly made a much-needed stop in a sari shop to purchase acceptable Indian attire. Then we continued our pilgrimage throughout the afternoon. We sat with a revered swami, whose primary message was: Serve and see all as God. May all beings find God's Realization. Throughout the day, Angena, our remarkable spiritual guide, continued with her stories while creating a beautiful bond of friendship and spiritual connection with all of us. The story of another goddess; Lakshmi, got my attention.

---

12.   Kali is the fearful and ferocious form of the mother goddess. She assumed the form of a powerful goddess and became popular with the composition of the Devi Mahatmya, a text of the fifth and sixth centuries AD.

[13]Goddess Lakshmi, also known as Shri, is personified not only as the goddess of fortune and wealth but also as an embodiment of loveliness, grace, and charm. She is worshipped as a goddess who grants both worldly prosperity as well as liberation from the cycle of life and death.

Lore has it that Lakshmi arose out of the sea of milk, the primordial cosmic ocean, bearing a red lotus in her hand. Each member of the Divine triad—Brahma, Vishnu, and Shiva (creator, preserver, and destroyer respectively)—wanted to have her for himself. Shiva's claim was refused for he had already claimed the Moon, Brahma had Saraswati, so Vishnu claimed her, and she was born and reborn as his consort during all of his ten incarnations. Though retained by Vishnu as his consort, Lakshmi remained an avid devotee of Lord Shiva. An interesting legend surrounds her devotion to this god. Every day Lakshmi had a thousand flowers plucked by her handmaidens, and she offered them to the idol of Shiva in the evening. One day, counting the flowers as she offered them, she found that there were two less than a thousand. It was too late to pluck any more for evening had come and the lotuses had closed their petals for the night. Lakshmi thought it inauspicious to offer less than a thousand. Suddenly she remembered that Vishnu had once described her breasts as blooming lotuses. She decided to offer them as the two missing flowers. Lakshmi cut off one breast and placed it with the flowers on the altar. Before she could cut off the other, Shiva, who was extremely moved by her devotion, appeared before her and asked her to stop. He then turned her cut breast into round, sacred bael fruit (Aegle marmelos) and sent it to Earth with his blessings to flourish near his temples.

The magic of the stories, the fragrance of rose petals, and the musical rhythm of India filled us with awe and magic. A moment of silence and deep smiles emerged and then we headed towards Ramakrishna Mission for another transformational adventure.

---

13.   The author researched for the complete Lakshmi story that Angena shared with the group. This story is printed with permission of www.exoticindia.com 2004

# Sri Ramakrishna Math

Love and Know God;
Serve God in Fellow Beings;
Respect all Religions.
~ *Sri Ramakrishna*

Sri Ramakrishna's life enables us to see God face to face.
No one can read the story of his life
without being convinced that God alone is real
and that all else is an illusion.
~ *Mahatma Gandhi*

Swami Vivekananda started the Ramakrishna Mission, or Math, in May 1897, but the origin of the mission can be traced back to the teenage years of Sri Ramakrishna's life. When Sri Ramakrishna had completed his spiritual practices, he had several realizations about himself and his future mission. He saw himself as a vessel, an instrument of the Divine Mother, who showed him that many devotees would come to him for spiritual guidance. The emblem of the mission is of remarkable beauty and very symbolic: It includes a rising sun symbolizing knowledge, wavy waters symbolic of work, a lotus flower which is the symbol of devotion surrounded by a serpent representing the awakened Kundalini energy, or dormant power within us all, and finally there is a swan, which represents the ultimate presence of the Divine also known as God. The main intention of the emblem was to represent the intention of Sri Ramakrishna's work, representing the importance of union through work and the self-realization process through the practice of Yoga, devotion, and knowledge.

To be honest, I knew very little about Swami Ramakrishna but was eager to feel the transmission of the temple. I was very attentive to this place, because the visit was planned by Mr. J. Joseph (God's angel). Since he had demonstrated that he was in the service of God and was following his heart to create a wonderful spiritual travel experience for us, I knew that visiting the mission was the perfect thing to do.

Inside the temple, hung a huge gallery of pictures of Ramakrishna's disciples. The energy there was very strong. My brainwaves and I entered into a peaceful state of bliss. At the back of the room where the image of Ramakrishna was, I sat down in the lotus position and meditated.

# Sri Sarada Devi

Whatever you may do, you have to give
Everybody in the household due attention
And consult their opinion.
You have to grant a little freedom and
Watch from a distance so that nothing may go very wrong.
*~ Sri Sarada Devi*

After a few moments, I stood and noticed that at the left side of the temple, which had a long corridor, was a shrine built of wood before a striking picture of a woman with dark brown hair that covered her chest as a veil of love. Devotees placed flowers in front of her. She was Sri Sarada Devi, known as the Mother, and recognized as the Shakti of Ramakrishna. I have heard that many people come to visit her shrine on the day of her Mahasamadhi.

The story is that Sri Sarada Devi was chosen by her family to marry Sri Ramakrishna but, when she encountered him, he told her that the only way he could see her was as the Divine Mother. He, indeed, was a real lover of the Divine in total selfless service to God as Mother and to humanity itself.

Sri Sarada Devi accepted him and became one of his disciples. Her devotion was grand and after the Mahasamadhi of Ramakrishna, Sri Sarada Devi was praised and visited by many disciples as well.

I felt a warm sensation running from the tip of my toes to the center of my heart! Her eyes, brown and deep, with her long black hair and gentle smile reminded me of the famous Mona Lisa and deeply stayed in my memory.

Her presence seemed more than a mere picture, and later, in time, I would reconnect with her in ways the mind would never expect.

# Swami Vivekananda

All love is expansion, all selfishness is contraction.
Love is therefore the only law of life.
He who loves, lives; he who is selfish is dying.
Therefore love for love's sake, because it is the law of life,
Just as you breathe to live.
~ *Swami Vivekananda*

My attention and curiosity was drawn toward a second picture close to Ramakrishna's Shrine. It pictured a handsome, dark-skinned man dressed in impeccable white with big black eyes whose name was Swami Vivekananda. He had been manifesting already for me, through e-mails, books, and even fliers! Yet, I knew very little of him except that he was chosen to continue Ramakrishna's message. Stories say he had an amazing power of mind. He developed many centers in India and promoted education for all. During our twenty-day pilgrimage in India, I often received pictures of him from others.

The name Vivekananda, however, triggered the memory of someone who I considered to be my first meditation teacher. My interest in Swami Vivekananda was really motivated by the one who introduced me in beautiful and intense ways to the concepts of meditation, conscious living, intention, and focus.

My first teacher had been a powerful catalyst for me. He not only delighted me with his stories, but being around him was a fun and sometimes difficult experience, including many ego-dissolving opportunities. Slowly and surely I came to the realization that everything always happens for a good reason and something new was always available to learn. He is a modern meditation master who experienced in his early years many metanormal states that led him to bliss. He lived for many years in India with Paramahansa Muktananda (one of the most recognized Eastern Masters of our era), where he was initiated as a Vedic monk. In his autobiography, he narrates that before being ordained by Muktananda, he saw Vivekananda himself and later received his swami name, which also happened to be, of course, Swami Vivekananda.

My first teacher remained in my awareness my entire visit to the Ramakrishna Math. Nothing but love and gratitude emerged with the remembrance of what he represented in my evolution as a human being. I still can smell his fragrance, a deep and intensely oriental fragrance, and the gratitude of his teachings will always reverberate in my heart.

While meditating at the temple, an ancient memory came back to me. I was sixteen years old, and my room at that time was a living altar. Everywhere there were deities, saints, and icons of God in His many forms. I had a special area for a collection of Buddhas, where I lit incense everyday. I had a Jesus section, a holy Mother section including the Virgin of Guadalupe, and a St. Francis collection. My room was my prayer place and refuge. In the Buddhist corner, I had a special book—*The Life and Teachings of Swami Vivekananda.*

I was far from knowing that six years later I would be meeting my first meditation teacher whose name would be Swami Vivekananda. Ten years after that, I would be inside the Mission Vivekananda in India, founded more than one hundred years ago. The memory delivered this next thought in me: *Everything in life is a beautiful game that dances along with you, entertains you for one main purpose: love, love, and more love.*

After connecting to the energy of Vivekananda, remembering with gratitude my first meditation teacher, and being amazed at the play of love as I walked through the hall, I took a good look at the pictures of the disciples of Ramakrishna. As a spiritual tourist, I read every explanation underneath each picture. All except for one—the image caught my attention so intensely. The picture had a young man, in his 40s probably, that looked more Westerner than Indian to me. A tingling sensation suddenly traveled through my spinal cord when my friend, Bhakti, blurted out exactly what my mind was thinking. "Ivonne, look! He looks exactly like Prema Baba Swamiji!" The resemblance was very strong. His eyes and mouth looked literally the same, the look of compassion, deep wisdom, and love was there, too. Not only were his physical features similar, but his name, Swami Premananda (Ecstatic Love), was similar, too. In less than one minute, another leela, a Hindu term for the Divine and eternal play of God.

# Swami Premananda

Can one become a great devotee of God simply by dancing
and jumping or by quoting plentifully from the scriptures?
What is wanted is freedom from selfishness—freedom from egotism.
Mere talk will not do; this is an age of action.
~ *Swami Premananda*

Swami Premananda received his name from Swami Vivekananda. Over the years, he served most lovingly in all endeavors he performed. He became an inspiration for young people in volunteering to serve society. He was a very humble being with many spiritual attainments, but he never praised himself for them. He died, or transcended his physical form, when a deadly disease manifested for him on July 30, 1918.

Premananda used to teach and demonstrate with his actions. He used to say:

> *To follow the Master means to practice what he taught; otherwise, nobody can advance by just offering a few flowers or through some momentary sentimental outbursts. Not mere theory; actualize it. There has been enough talk and writing. Put the books aside and let your actions speak. The poor, the weak, the fallen, and the ignorant—all these you have to make your own. And yet I warn you, that in loving one section of society you must not become hateful of the other, the rich.*

I found his teaching to be very similar to that of beloved Prema Baba Swamiji. Although we can never be sure if Prema Baba is a reincarnation of Premananda or not, one thing is for sure: Existence was playing divine games with us. My delight and recognition of it recharged my love batteries. My heart was expanding even more! I felt very grateful to be in God's game!

We walked for a little while around the Ramakrishna Math, meditated a bit, and then went back to our white Quail for the next Angena-guided adventure in India. Our destination was a place that no regular tourist could have ever found—Samratchana House. We had an appointment there, which our travel angel, Mr. J. Joseph, set up for us with Guru Sivashankar Baba.

# The Mysterious Appointment

A gentle hand may lead an elephant with a single hair.
*~ Persian proverb*

When we arrived, Angena and our driver spoke with the ladies who opened the door. After many minutes of dancing heads, they told us that the guru was not inside and they were performing [14]*arati*, a temple ritual where a fire on a plate is respectfully waved in front of a deity in a clockwise direction in its glorification as a fire blessing. They graciously invited us in. A short and skinny woman with a smile shining with the opportunity to receive guests approached and gave me an apple blessed by the guru. It is said that holy food blessed by the guru himself can trigger the most ecstatic and meditative experiences in the disciple; it is also known in India as Prasad. She anointed us with a [15]*tilak mark*, a vermilion mark applied with a powdery substance named *kum kum* on the forehead with the religious significance of opening the third eye to receive the guru wisdom, and we felt more than blessed.

We came out of the house accompanied by the beautiful devotees, smiling and saying farewell. One of them invited us to come in the morning to the ashram at 7 AM to meet with Sivashankar Baba. Then Angena took us to meet with Maharishi Sri Bharadwaj Swamigal. A holy celebration was going on in town, and the narrow and crowded streets were closed. The opportunity to walk presented itself again. Barefoot, we walked to a small house/ashram on the street Gangai Nagar. On our way we saw the beggars on the streets, children and elder begging for one or two rupees, young girls selling garlands of roses and jasmine, and a short man in a corner selling postcards from India. The horns of cars trying to get in to the closed street accompanied our walk as music until we arrived at the guru's home.

A full load of shoes was outside the door. Being barefoot is a sign of respect in holy places and to saints and gurus. A man received us and told us to come up the stairs and sit and wait. Angena, who also happened to be a great spiritual friend, had a conversation with this young man and then gave us some papers. The forms asked our names and for us to write down our problem or request. I simply wrote my name and that my request was "Only to meet him as a new friend." When our time arrived for darshan (the viewing and conversation with a spiritual Master), we were asked to enter a small living room. We sat down on a red car-

---

14. The meaning of arati found in http://www.kamat.org/glossary.asp?WhoID=322
15. Data from http://hindunet.org/tilak/

pet; the place had no chairs except the big red one of the guru. Pictures of ancient sages were hanging on the walls. The room resembled the humble space where a renunciant of the material world lived. Sri Bharadwaj was sitting and looking at us. We sat and Angena began promoting us. The guru smiled and asked questions about us. Then he kept smiling and smiling...and so did we. We really had no requests. All of us were happy—blissful, in fact. It's not every day you get to visit Guru Land!

Sri Bharadwaj is well known in India as a healer. Angena told us that many people request to see him to resolve big problems and heal from illnesses. She said it was very hard to see him in a private setting as we did. Then I asked if he had anything to say to us. He replied, "No." He smiled, we smiled, and then he said that he would always be with us, and that he predicted great spiritual work in our paths.

Then, like children, we received gifts—pictures of him and his father Parmahamsa Srimath Bhuvaneswari Swamigal. We said farewell and left with gifts, with joy, and with inner God fulfillment.

© Bharadwaj Swamigal, who received the group privately and
announced for them special blessings and predicted great spiritual work
in their path.

# The Divine Message
## Sharadambal Temple
## (Also known as the Turapaty-Thirumala-Balally)

Life isn't about finding yourself. Life is about creating yourself.
*~ George Bernard Shaw*

We parked the car in front of the temple and left our shoes inside. We were about to experience our first "Dare to cross the street in India adventure." The street was crowded with people and cows who seemed invisible to the car drivers who were just moving as ants will do around sugar. There were no stop signs or red lights…except for the inner intuition of each pedestrian. The people from India were fine with it; they crossed the street as if there were no cars at all. The women would laugh if by chance a car would probably hit them. Everything seemed surreal and intense from my view, but, at the same time, I felt the invitation once more to trust and prove that my reflexes worked! We finally did it; we crossed our first street in India, although when we arrived safely on the other side, our breathing was rapid and our hearts were racing.

When we entered the Sharadambul Temple, a white structure embellished with sculptures of gods and goddesses everywhere, it looked gray from pollution and crowded as if a baseball game was going on. Instead of sports what was happening was a puja, a ceremony where fire is blessed with different ingredients and then is used as a blessing for all in the temple. Angena once again managed to take us to the front with the priests. There were many people waiting to receive a blessing from Agni (the Sacred Fire) and receive *prasad* and a tilak mark.

The chanting of the Vedic mantras, the temple, and the people transported me to a deep place of silence, even though I was surrounded by noise. One of the Brahmins offered me the fire. I placed my hands above the bowl, "scooped up" the blessings, and symbolically "draped" my body with it. Then he gave us lassi to drink, a sweet beverage made out of yogurt and spices like cardamom, clove, and cumin, kum kum (a red powdery substance) to take for our foreheads, and some cooked rice to eat. All the rituals were fine, yet my bliss stopped cold when food or drink was offered to me in the temples. All of the negative data about impure food or water really triggered doubts in me whether to take it or not. My spiritual beliefs arose strongly, and I wanted to break through my limitations, so I ate and drank whatever was given to me in holy places.

I felt so energized, like if I had slept eight hours or more, and felt totally refreshed. The air somehow was lighter, and the sky looked clearer to my eyes. I appreciated the colors of creation, and I felt grateful toward all the people who were smiling and treating us so beautifully. On our way out of the temple, a man and a young woman approached my dear friend Alex (Akshmilanandaji) and me. The man acknowledged the beautiful energy he felt from Alex, and then the young lady said to me, "I am so proud of you!" My mind completely stopped. Just a couple of minutes before I was thinking, "Oh, dear Divine Mother, I am grateful I broke through my fear of coming to India. Thank you. Please send me a sign that you heard me." And then, a moment later, this beautiful young girl was smiling at me and saying, "I am so proud of you." Tears filled my eyes with joy, overwhelmed with the experience, and my mind couldn't function very well with practical reasoning. The man, who happened to be her father, said something wonderful to me and gave me a picture of his guru, Swami Vivekananda.

Alex and I then joined in saying one of our favorite mantras during this magical journey. We walked out of the temple, intoxicated with bliss. Oh, no! We needed to cross the street again. This time I didn't even think about it. I just walked across. As soon as I did I remembered 10 words from the Tao Te Ching: "*Whoever can see through all fear will always be safe.*"

# Siddha Yogi Sivashankar Baba
## September 19

Start the Day with LOVE;
Spend the Day with LOVE;
Fill the Day with LOVE;
End the Day with LOVE;
This is the way to God.
~ *Sivashankar Baba*

If you gain God and lose everything else,
What is it that you have lost?
If you lose God and gain everything else,
What is it that you have gained?
~ *Sivashankar Baba*

We woke up very early to be ready at 6:30 to go with Angena to the [16]Sam-ratchana Ashram. The ashram, an area of five or six acres, was beautifully land-scaped with jasmine, banyan trees, gardenias, and different local plants, and there were shrines and altars of all different religions and cultures all made with exact precision. Along the walking path were lots of "Messages of the Guru" signs: FOLLOW NO ONE. ALL IS LOVE. Many children filled the ashram, and I felt the joyful energy coming from their sweet smiles and radiant energy. Girls were sew-ing flower garlands as carefully as an artist would, and people watched us watch-ing them.

On our walk through the center, we stopped to pray in each of the temples, Muslim, Catholic, Islamic, and Hindu. Then awareness began expanding inside my heart, for the more I prayed, the more I felt the place filled with peace; silence as in being on top of a mountain by myself with no other sounds except those in nature. I felt magical energy everywhere and prayed for all souls to be united in the religion of love no matter the divine diversity of spiritual and religious choices. We arrived then at a place where many people were preparing for the ceremony of the day that the guru would guide. They told us Sivashankar would be performing. A group of musicians was singing beautiful *bhajans* (chants to the Divine). The ashram was preparing to celebrate The Festival of Lights. Angena enlightened us with more stories and explanations of what was happening. If

16.   Located in Tamil Nadu. www.samratchana.org

there is one occasion that is all joy and all jubilation for one and all—the young and the old, men and women—for the entire Hindu world, it is [17]Deepaavali, the Festival of Lights. Even the humblest of huts will be lighted by a row of earthen lamps. Crackers resound and light up the earth and the sky. The faces of boys and girls flow with a rare charm in their dazzling hues and colors. Illumination—Deepotsavas—in temples and all sacred places of worship and on the banks of rivers symbolize the scattering of spiritual radiance all around from these holy centers.

Angena said that this festival was very important for her and all people in India for their [18]*Karma* would also receive the Divine light and make them freer.

While stories and contemplation were happening, a man had prepared a special place—seats of honor—for us. I really preferred to sit on the floor like everybody else, but the gesture was made with such pleasure to serve that we couldn't refuse.

They announced that Sivashankar was about to arrive. We took our places and listened to the mantras begin. A well-dressed man in a beautiful long silk brown shirt and off-white silk pants stood in front of us. He looked at us as if he had X rays on his eyes. Everyone was in silence, and then while standing in front of Akshmilanandaji and me, he entered into a trance-like state. His body began to assume different deity postures, and *mudras* (prayerful hand gestures) scanned our energy. His eyes changed colors from brown to green, and from blue to gray. I was not amazed; I was just allowing myself to experience the moment. Then he opened his eyes and said he would meet with us after the ceremony and said to us: *You are Good People.*

He performed all the ritual blessings and then gave *prasad* (sweet rice blessed by the guru) to the children of the ashram. Their little hands were eager to catch a candy from the guru. We were delighted and impressed. Children from three to nine years old were chanting beautifully. No one was telling them what to do or yelling at them, "Sit down, be quiet!" They were naturally flowing with the energy, and instinct told them what to do.

Watching this interaction gave me a profound moment of insight. In the West, we strive for conscious education. We read books about parenting. We focus on skills and learning, and we offer the best developmental toys. Yet we

---

17.   www.hindunet.com

18.   The word karma is derived from the Sanskrit root 'kri,' meaning 'to do,' implying that all action is karma. Technically, the term incorporates both an action and its consequence. When we confront a dilemma, namely the relative impurity and purity of an action, what determines the nature of the karma is the will or intention behind an act. www.hinduwebsite.com

usually fail miserably for all our effort. However, I was in India experiencing a natural respect that adults have for children and saw what we would call "appropriate behavior" without programming or excessive information. The guru approached the singers, and suddenly the mantra singing changed into "Happy Birthday" in English! The ashram was celebrating the birthday of one of the little girls that lived in the ashram that was turning eight. Sivashankar gave her some gifts, and then the feast began. As honored guests, food was brought to us where we were sitting. We were served a plate with steamed rice, vegetables with creamy tomato, tamarind sauce, and a chapatti, and it was wonderful. It was breakfast for us, and one more blessing for me.

After the feast, Sivashankar came over to us and this time, standing in front of Bhakti and Govinda, he screamed something. His posture began to shift in the most perfect movement I've ever seen. With the grace of a ballerina, his arms were raised in prayer posture, his legs seemed lighter, and then his hands moved and seemed to hold a flute in his hands, his feet turned blue color, and his eyes turned yellow, and suddenly his whole body became the body of Krishna. I swear to you his posture movements and his energy felt as if I was being struck with lightning on my spine and chest; it was unbelievable! (Another of our mantras!) Yet, it was only unbelievable for a programmed mind. It was happening in front of my eyes. The energy felt so strong, my body got locked up in bliss. Gratitude, once again, was my experience.

Then he said to us, "Drink some tea and then come with me." I was so excited that I almost couldn't drink my tea fast enough. While we walked with him, he spoke perfect English and told us how his ashram worked.

His center rendered positive-oriented services that are totally free. Anyone who came to Samratchana was given free food between 11 AM and 4 PM. On Pournami days, wholesome lunches and snacks were provided throughout the entire day. The center also offered free food distribution, free medical care, free legal care, and free classes in cartoon animation, tailoring, embroidery, textile painting, typing and shorthand, screen printing, journalism, foreign language, and spoken English.

They also provided sponsorship for travel and tourism, foreign-trade management, hotel management, marketing, and international banking classes. They offer free summer camps for students on spirituality, free music training—vocal and instrumental—free Bharatha Natyam dance classes, free karate and Yoga classes, free Reiki, Veda, and meditation classes. Their computer classes were offered at a very nominal cost.

Samratchana has adopted two villages, Vengaleri and Alathur, near Thirupporur in Tamil Nadu and provides facilities ranging from free education to free medical camps, bringing light into the lives of those villagers. Samratchana is the only place where you will find people moving as members of the same family, investing total care in each other, regardless of age, creed, gender or background. Samratchana is not just another institution; it is the Center for Self-Realization. It is the model of the Universal Family.

While walking along with Baba listening to him, I felt pretty much at ease. His voice was joyful and deep, his fatherly nature was like a strong and yet subtle hug. He kept looking at our eyes as he spoke and laughed as often as he was breathing. His energy was an open invitation to love without judgments and expectations. I was happy to meet such a beautiful human being who was evidently doing great work through assisting many people in practical life matters and helping them find God's Realization! His sharing was not only in words; it was based in the reality of his actions and manifestations.

We finally arrived at a house (I think it was his home). A white structure decorated with painted garlands on the outside. Inside, everything was beautiful. The furniture was made out of leather. A long wood dining table was at the center of the room. The decorations included some plastic inflatable toys that seasoned the room with laughter and lightheartedness. Pictures of Sivashankar were the main art hung on walls, and the fragrance of sandalwood incense was pure delight for the senses. He asked us to come into his puja room.

# The Puja

Ritual of adoration,
Homage to the Divine.
Heart offerings, prayerful whispers,
Soul burning as divine incense
offered to a deity that reflects the God within.
~ *Ivonne Delaflor*

Sivashankar Baba invited us to sit down in his Puja Room (a place specially designed for sacred rituals commonly offered to a deity with a certain intention and purpose). It was beautiful and refined, although small. The five of us, along with Sivashankar, fit perfectly. In the center was an altar with deities where the puja, which included burning of candles, incense, and offerings, is performed. All the implements needed were right in front of us.

When the puja began and the fire started taking form, I couldn't close my eyes. Something in me wanted to see everything that was happening—at least what my ordinary eyes could see. Puja is a ceremony offered to the deities, an adoration ritual that is believed to have intense powers of healing, transformation, fulfillment, and purification.

During the ritual, Sivashankar poured *ghee* (clarified butter) into the fire, then milk, then honey and many other holy substances. The fire was tall. I thought my mind was playing tricks on me for I saw forms in the flames. First, I saw a man who seemed like Krishna to me and then other Hindu deity images. I disregarded these visions, thinking they were just my imagination. When the puja came to completion, I felt purified and deeply connected to Sivashankar. After the ritual, he requested one of his assistants bring us his family photo album so he could share with us his experiences. When he opened it up and showed us the pictures, our jaws literally dropped!

# The Sacred Family

*All is possible in a child's imagination
and in a trustful and open heart.
~ Ivonne Delaflor*

The album that SivaShankar shared with us as his personal album was loaded with pictures that had been taken of him throughout the years. In some, his fire puja would take the form of the gods and goddesses—Ganesha, Shiva, or Krishna dancing in the fire! All the deities were perfectly formed with fire. I was totally shocked. No thoughts were running wild in my mind, disbelief disappeared, and the misunderstanding of what my eyes saw was as powerful as meditating three hours in a row. In all the pictures, a light surrounded him. Sivashankar explained that these pictures were always taken during a ceremony, a puja or a meditative *samadhi* (God-realized state of consciousness).

What I liked most was his naturalness in sharing his "family album" with us. The Divine representations were his family members. What is so strange about that? I mean, many people have pictures of Uncle Bob or Grandma or the sunset! Baba had his pictures taken with Ganesha, Krishna, and Kali. Is that so strange?

Sivashankar also told us that he could travel through outer body experiences very easily and that he had sometimes been seen at two places at the same time. This well-studied phenomenon is practiced by yogis around the world. I told him that we would be delighted to invite him to Mexico and that he could travel either light speed or on a regular plane. He laughed and smiled!

Then he invited us to stay with him the next time we came to India. He told us that we should not be looking for long-bearded guru types. We had everything inside ourselves already. "Besides," he said, "you could stay here with me. No need to pay anything, donate anything, or give anything. Just allow yourselves to receive."

Afterward he gave us gifts of pens, and we took a picture with him, secretly hoping that his "family members" might show up in our picture. His car was already outside waiting for his next appointment at the hospital on the ashram. I longed for some reason to stay with him. Angena kept reminding us that we needed to keep on moving since we had a plane to catch that afternoon. As we drove away, I looked back to see printed on his car a sign that said, "God's Car." I smiled and closed my eyes.

We dropped Angena off and her farewell message to us was one of gratitude. She said being a guide for us had been a very spiritual experience for her—one of the best moments in her career.

Before leaving the hotel, Devananda and I went back to the room to pick up our things and to mediate for a short time in gratitude. The man who had cleaned the room knocked on our door. He was a beautiful man, probably twenty-three years old or younger, very thin, deep black eyes, and very dark and soft hair. He said that he knew I was a Swamini, and he wanted my blessings and the transmission of my Shakti or yogi powers. Struck by this, I prayed inside to know how to respond with humble words to this young man who believed I had something to give him. He requested that I put a *tilak mark* (using kum kum, the red powdery substance) on his forehead, and then I prayed with him. My mind immediately went searching for Prema Baba Swamiji, asking, "Why did you ordain me as a Swamini? What am I supposed to do? Why me?" And the answer came: *Follow your heart!*

I did. I had a postcard with beautiful Mayan angels created by one of our friends. I wrote on the card the first words my heart dictated: "Find God within. Recognize your power inside and remember that the grandest teacher above all is LOVE ITSELF."

Then I gave him the address of Sivashankar Baba's ashram since he was demonstrating a deep desire for a teacher and a guide in a human form. I also gave him some gifts and the apple that Sivashankar had given me. The young man then bowed at my feet, and I bowed at his. Trembling in humbleness in the power of the experience, I couldn't help but wonder about the responsibility that this event implied in my life!

Siva Shankar Baba with Swami Govinda & Bhaktiananda.
© Mastery Life A.C

# 2

## *The Divine Mother*

Feminine Divine Energy;
Your womb feeds the soul of the Universe.
And in your nurturing arms
We uplift our spirits
Becoming One with Creation.

*~ Ivonne Delaflor*

# The Mother's Magical Embrace

"Just as a doctor gives different dosages or even different medications to patients with the same ailment according to their constitution, so does a guru prescribe different methods to different people to reach the same goal. Spirituality is the practical science of life. Apart from taking us to the ultimate goal of self-realization, it also teaches us the nature of the world, and how to understand life, and live fully in the best way possible."

~ Amma

After only forty-five minutes into our journey to Trivandrum, the pilot announced that we were to land. It was difficult for me to understand this English translation they were giving, but I assumed that since we were landing, we had arrived, although I was expecting a two-hour flight. When we landed, my friends and I took our things and began to line up to deplane. Some passengers followed us, but many others didn't. One of my friends asked the steward, "Is this Trivandrum?"

He laughed and said, "No, the next stop is yours!"

We all burst out laughing! It was one of the most ecstatically funny, laughing meditations for all of us. And it was a sign to be more attentive and to keep on celebrating the unexpected moments of life.

When we landed for the second time, we made sure we had arrived at our destination. We expected someone to pick us up at 5:05 PM, but our plane had been delayed. We waited a little and then Mr. Vishnu, sent by our friend Gautam, arrived. Gautam was the one who sent me an invitation to come to India for his teacher Ammachi's birthday celebration. Though we hadn't met personally, my heart felt the recognition of my dear Soul mate, God, working through him to create a wonderful experience for us.

We got into the car and managed to fit the suitcases—some on the roof, some inside. From Trivandrum, we were to drive two hours to arrive at the Amritapuri International Ashram located in the Kollam District in Kerala.

When we were in Chennai, the driving was fast. Traffic signs were usually ignored but that was okay, the traffic in the city was slow. But Vishnu, our driver, was about to introduce us to a whole new dimension of trust and surrender. The narrow roads were bumpy at the beginning of our trip. As we drove, the views began to shift from city structures to wild jungle landscape. The sky began to darken, and we discovered that the headlights on the car didn't work. No problem, right? Cars were zooming around us, fast and faster. The road was narrow and very dark. Absolutely no road signs were seen. Amazingly, I felt at ease and even went to sleep. I gave my trust to the fact that if Vishnu (one of the three aspects of the Hindu Trinity) was driving, I didn't have to worry.

My dear friends Govinda and Bhakti, though, had some intense moments. During this Bollywood (Bombay + Hollywood-style movie) action car chase driving frenzy, my friend Alex reminded me of a dream he had. He was in a school bus, and the driver was driving sort of India-like, and suddenly the bus went down a road directly to the edge of a precipice. In his dream, he heard the words, "Trust in God." As he narrated the dream, Vishnu's driving became more intense, the honking and the rapid wheel movements. It was surreal! I was enjoying it all and amazed at my relaxation. Often spontaneously, my friends and I would begin to sing *bhajans* (Sanskrit mantras) while riding in the car. Sometimes our focus was acutely attuned with India's powerful energy, and we couldn't imagine that our journey could get any better, or worse!

We finally arrived at the ashram at 8:30 in the evening. Lots of people were lined up, chanting. The ashram was full. Something special seemed to be happening, but first we went to the office to announce our arrival and ask for instructions. We were asked to wait. Then people moved very fast and attentively. A woman from Spain cleared my puzzled mind, saying that they were waiting for Amma. My friends and I stood exactly where we were and, walking toward us in the middle of thousands of people, there she was—the holy woman whose invitation initiated in me the power to travel to India. She walked close to the people who stretched their arms out with the hope that Amma would touch them.

She stopped to greet us; an auspicious welcome. The first person we met at the ashram was the guru herself. The second person we encountered was Gautam, a young man with wise eyes, a passion for service, and a beautiful smile. He assisted us beyond expectations. He took us to our rooms, showed us the facilities, and welcomed us at all times with so much joy. With his big white smile, he reflected the happiness of one who is fulfilled upon finding his mission or destiny—the joy of being a disciple of Amma.

We were assigned rooms on the ashram on the 11th floor. Thank God it had an elevator because our luggage, especially mine, was really heavy from all the things I thought I needed to bring to India. Silently, I prayed with gratitude for the creation of technology! Bhakti, Deva, and I stayed in one room, and in the adjoining room, Govinda and Akshmil.

We held a meditation session that night in the guest room. Ame (the Source or Higher Self whom I channel) was directing us toward focusing on creating a fulfilling, truthful experience. Gautam knocked on the door and invited us to walk with him. Although it was very late, Akshmilanandaji and I were willing to go.

Gautam walked us through the ashram, which looked like a university campus to my eyes. Big buildings were seen, including a traditional pink-colored South India temple, with a huge room where chanting and meditations were held every day. The ashram, as we walked, was less crowded now in the evening. Most people were in their dormitory rooms. Some devotees were still working. I could tell they were tired—the bags under their eyes gave that away—but their blissful look was dominant. They were the White Angels, as I began to call them, with their white clothes, white smiles, and an angelic mood of always looking for an opportunity to serve.

He showed us the whole ashram, which included the house of Amma, a simple, humble structure inside the ashram that probably had only one room and a small kitchen. The energy was indeed embracing us. The sharing of Gautam regarding the joy of being of service to Amma stayed in our hearts.

# The Positive Child Called Amma
## The Mother of Eternal Bliss
## September 21

Just as hatred and vengefulness exist in the mind,
peace and love can also exist in the mind.
~ Amma

Meditation at the main temple inside the ashram was at 8 AM. Many people were gathered. We went for breakfast to find a long line of people requesting special meals. The food was fantastic, delicious chapattis, coconut rice, tea masala flavored with cardamom, and oatmeal with different spices. They had different options to choose from, both Indian meals and a Western cafeteria. I could barely eat anything at all. Filled with an energy that was like food and like sleep and like everything. I was "full" already. Praying before our meals became more joyous. I was grateful to be there. I prayed in silence, thanking the Divine for the precious breath that allowed me to be alive and experience this magical India journey.

We had been invited the night before to meet with Amma at 11 AM. We went for our appointment at the exact time but had to wait for an hour. A swami, Shubamrita, appeared and said, "Come with me! Come, come! Amma is giving darshan where she gathers with her disciples for a question-and-answer session, followed by the chants of bhajans and the offering of gifts from guru to disciple and vice versa, completing with the powerful and well-known embrace that Amma gives to all through her loving hug. And I've saved you a space close to her."

Rushing, we followed him up a spiral snail staircase, leaving our shoes behind. Focused on going fast, I barely knew where was I going. I completely lost all sense of direction. Between many people, he opened up a space for us to walk. I was asked to sit in front of a three-dimensional figure who appeared before my eyes. It was Amma.

My mind completely stopped.

AMMA picture (c) 2003 MA Center, Castro Valley, California.
Used with permission.

# Questions to the Mother

Lending a helping hand to a neglected soul,
feeding the hungry, giving the sad and dejected a
compassionate smile—this is the language of love.
Let us focus on what we can give to others,
for only then will we experience deep joy and fulfillment in life.
~ *Amma*

Amma was such a beautiful woman, her long black hair, her smile as radiant as the sun, her eyes melted as she tastefully and carefully looked to each one of the people in the room. She stopped my mind with her compassionated energy. I can see vividly once again the way she looked at me, her eyes gazed through mine as a powerful laser beam, scanning my energy with hers, giving total focus an attention to my eyes reflected on hers and smiling while nodding her head with a welcoming gesture. When I sat down in front of her, I saw her form like the 3-D movie theaters that you need special glasses to see the images with. The multidimensionality of existence was present in that moment, and I could see it with my ordinary eyes! My mind had no expectations at all. It was a clear instant of realization for me.

The *Darshan* began, and Swami Ramakrishnananda chanted OM three times. We all chanted along with him. Slowly I began to gain some "consciousness" in regard to where I was, whom I was with, and who I was! We were inside the main temple of the ashram, which only decoration and deities in the moment visible to the eye were the thousands of people inside the temple where we had mediated early that morning. Amma began chanting a *bhajan* that my friends and I fell in love with, "Govinda Gopala," dedicated to Lord Krishna as a child (Gopala) and as an adolescent (Govinda). It was uplifting and beautiful. And the energy in the room from all the people singing along with her was warming the place not only with heat, but also with love.

After the chanting, Amma requested that people ask her questions. The beautiful, smiley Brahmachari Shubamrita translated every word that Amma said into English, and then I would translate it into Spanish for my friends. The place was very crowded! A human form occupied every single space. I then heard a Swami saying there were 2,500 people inside the temple. Where did all these people come from? What was the energy that attracted them so much?

A woman asked Amma why she couldn't stop crying whenever she was in Amma's presence. The woman, with a child-like energy, created a smile in me.

Watching her faith, devotion, and compassion toward her guru really moved my heart. It made me think of all the thirsty believers in our world who are in search of a deeper life, understanding, and crying out for *love*, the Master of them all.

Amma responded to the woman's question, and I translated for my friends. She told the lady that hers were *bhakti* tears, healing and devotional tears, and a cleansing process for her mind. Amma also said jokingly that tears in meditative states were signs of greater spiritual development, but if you cried about everything all the time, then you should check with a doctor about signs of depression. Everybody laughed. She was funny, quick, and focused with her words while transmitting a beautiful maternal energy that was warm and nurturing to all. She kept looking at all of us with the eyes of a mother. Her smile was bigger and brighter! And her energy was that of a child, full of stamina, and with grand joy for service.

Then a young man from New York said, "I just want to thank you for all you give to us, for all the service you do. Rather than asking something for me, I just want to thank you." Amma's deep big brown eyes looked at him with the same gratitude he was bestowing upon her. She was serving him as a mirror of his beauty. This man caught my attention. His energy was familiar. In the days to come, we would meet again.

A woman asked about Jesus and his sacrifice for the world. Amma began to respond, and the energy became more and more blissful. Ecstasy was apparent, the faces of all in the room were like hypnotized by Amma's loving presence; tears for some, smiles for many. The view was uplifting—very uplifting—but I couldn't really give any meaning to the answer Amma was giving her. Nevertheless, I kept on translating automatically. Suddenly, my friend Bhakti said to me, "Ivonne, you are translating Amma!" And I said, "Yes, that's what I am doing." Then she repeated "Amma!"

My jaw dropped I had indeed been translating her before the English translation was even given! How did that happened? How could I have done that? I didn't know the language she was speaking (Malayalam). It was one of the South Indian dialects. I speak English, Spanish, and understand a little French and that's all. What was happening to me? Of course as soon as my mind got into the wondering of how, the translation stopped and, once again, I needed to wait to hear the English translation.

This insight and deep contemplation will stay with me today and every day of my life. If all human beings were immersed in the bliss of love, in the complete trust that everything is perfect in existence, there would be no divisions, no different languages, and no differences at all. There would only be one word and one language—the language of love. I was amazed and in an altered state of aware-ness. What was real? What was not? Who cared? The moment was absolutely amazing.

The last question was from a man asking if it was all right to meet with other gurus and if it would not disturb the relationship he had with her, his *Satguru* (the Master who guides you to your supreme consciousness, toward God's Real-ization). Amma's answer was simple. Do whatever you like. Meeting with other gurus is not of any harm. But you should keep only to one *Satguru*. If you don't, the mind gets confused with too much information.

After the question-and-answer session, people were asked to form a line to receive *darshan* from Amma—to receive a hug and *prasad* (an exchange of blessed gifts). I took a deep breath for I was the second in the line of thousands.

My turn came. I was assisted by Br. Dayamrita to get closer to Amma. Such intensity! She pulled me strongly into her arms. I was astonished. I never expected to touch her. Once again, the spontaneous nature of reality was playing with me. Her hug was a complete delight! I cannot say that I melted or felt scin-tillating lights but, with huge gratitude, I felt that she was doing such an amazing job of serving as a guide, a mother, giving hope and relief to so many people. Internally I said to God. "Wow, it is so good to meet with all your workers of light!"

Then Amma began repeating a Sanskrit name for me. I don't remember it, but the warmth of it was amazing. I wanted to understand it, but the energy was stronger, and I gave up trying to understanding the meaning. Br. Shubamrita introduced me to her. He said, "This is Ivonne, the lady from Mexico." She pulled me back again into her arms and kissed me this time. Then I gave her a gift I had brought from Cancun—the drawings of the ninety children in the cele-bration of Peace.

She was delighted! She hugged me strongly three or four times. I could feel her excitement and, in the midst of a huge crowd waiting and hoping to receive the hug of the Mother, she began telling me eagerly that they had done the same project or something very similar in India with the schools her ashram had estab-lished. Then Amma told me that my work with children was a blessing that I should continue no matter what. She asked me to sit behind her and wait for her. Then she gave me an apple!

My mind began to whirl in its programmed thinking: "I hope this apple has been washed. Has it been disinfected? Again, I received an apple as *prasad*! First Shankar Baba and then Amma! Of course!" The manifestation of this second apple was evidence that either I could create a reality based on programming, or I could make the choice to believe that the blessing of a guru was far beyond any existent or nonexistent bug in the food. I chose the second option but, to be perfectly honest, I ate the apple later.

Everything happened so quickly! I (and my friends) sat down right behind her. The velocity in which she hugged each person in the room, the way she looked directly at their eyes, the constant giving and receiving of gifts, the volunteers keeping everything in order assisting people. While time for my eyes moved fast, it also seemed like it stopped. I was in a state of nothingness. How did Amma know about my work with children? Her aides had told her that I gave workshops, but she said things to me in that moment that I had not ever told anyone! How had she known? I sat behind her in the lotus position. Her assistants were precisely honoring and preparing all of the *prasad* that Amma gives to everyone at *darshan*. I was drawn to naturally begin to assist in preparing the sweets and collecting the gifts Amma was receiving from people. Everything unfolded so quickly. Yet, at the same time, "time" itself had stopped. I was inebriated with love from all the devotion and the energy, not only coming from Beloved Amma, but from all of her devotees, I felt dizzy as I merged in deep and warm joy that created a tingling sensation in my heart chakra and in the top of my head.

At my left side was a little girl from Japan assisting her mother in preparing the *darshan* gifts. She was being very playful with one of the devotees who was immersed in deep meditation. Her joy delighted me more, and a loud message kept repeating itself in my mind: *Serve the children of the world.*

I sat there watching Amma, bewildered from her strength and constancy. It took such energy to be able to hug each person with so much love, attention, and with the same joyful face! The devotees assisting her would change places now and then. They took turns, but Amma had no one else to do her "work." The darshan lasted I don't know how long—two, three, four hours? More than two thousand people! Amma was hugging, receiving gifts, and exchanging prayers and greetings all that time.

The more I sat there behind Amma, watching, the more drunk I became. All I could see were human beings all dressed in white, looking like angels. Was I in heaven? For sure, this moment felt like heaven, although it had nothing to do with any thought, expectation, or person. It had to do with what was happening in the moment. I just couldn't help but feel grateful to be...just be.

The *darshan* came to completion, and I knew already that Amma's request for me to stay there—to be there—had nothing to do with her wanting to have a spoken conversation with me afterward. Her invitation was to be in the moment.

She stood up, bowed to all the people, and walked away from the temple. I was filled with energy, my dizziness and my love for the Divine ever increasing.

There is one thing I need to make clear, however. I did not go to India looking for someone or something or to find a guru. I went to India because my heart pulled me to the adventure of it, because the invitation I received felt real. My beloved Soul mate, God, offered it to me. At this moment, I was in India and that was enough. All the extra unexpected events were an added blessing and miracle to the gift of life itself.

We walked away from Amma's temple intoxicated with bliss. My mind was very quiet. While we were walking, a sound arose—the reverberation of it came from everywhere and everyone. It was *OM*, the primordial reverberation and music of the Divine.

# Nectar from the Gods

He is the only adorable one to me: I have none other.
My tongue has left off impure words; it sings His glory day and night.
Whether I rise or sit down, I can never forget Him;
for the rhythm of His music beats in my ears.
Kabir says: "My heart is frenzied, and I disclose in my soul what is hidden.
I am immersed in that one great bliss which transcends all pleasure and pain."
*~ Kabir*

Food offered to God is free from unconscious vibrations that
might injure the individual in subtle ways.
Since food has subtle impact on the feelings and thoughts,
You have to be ever vigilant.
*~ Sai Sathya Sai Baba*

At the cafeteria, we prayed in silence and in gratitude for the food. My constant prayer is (and was): "Please God, BE the food I eat and the mouth I eat it with. Thank you."

After the prayer, I tried to put a small amount of rice into my mouth—maybe half a teaspoon. At the moment the food touched my mouth, a warm sensation of pleasure and ecstasy began to vibrate in my being. My mouth was full—but not full of food. I was eating nectar from the gods. The air that was inside my mouth gained structure and form. I tried to chew, but it kept dissolving. My ecstasy grew higher and higher. I was literally eating air. At moments the exhilaration delivered spontaneous sounds in me: Ahhhhh, Mmmmhhhh, Ohhhhhhh. Yes, the experience was orgasmic, in the most sublime and subtle way.

Then a burst of laughter from very deep inside of me arose. Everyone around me disappeared. I could not hear any noise or sounds of people talking. From time to time, I would stop chewing in order to contemplate the moment and ask myself, am I really here?

# Brahmachari Dayamrita

*Satsanga with Mahatmas, Sadhus, and the guru plays a tremendous part*
*in the attainment of quick spiritual progress.*
*~ Swami Sivananda*

We arrived at Br. Dayamrita's room at 3:30 sharp for a *satsang* with him, a session of questions and answers. A very tall man, in his 30s, born in India, he has been in the service of Amma for many years. He is in charge of the Amma Math, or ashram in California, and wanted to talk to us about the possibility of bringing Amma to Mexico.

His tall stature, long black beard, and orange robes created an outward mood of grand respect and seriousness. What a delight to find the wonderful child inside the orange robe of an eminently beautiful soul! We talked about our work in the *Mastery Life Organization,* and we shared experiences. His room was very simple—just a bed with a light red blanket, a sofa, and a little brown wooden table. On the walls hung pictures of Amma and Swami Amritaswarupananda, one of Amma's disciples who has been with her for twenty years. He is Amma's senior-most disciple.

My friend Alex (Akshmilanandaji) shared with Dayamrita his knowledge of Mayan astrology and did a chart for him. Then the Swami reached for his laptop, and he delighted us with his astrological Vedic wisdom and did a reading for both Alex and me. He told me that the work I was doing would be recognized worldwide and that I should persist in the service I was offering. He also said that in thirteen years I would become a renunciant from the world.

We were joking and laughing together, feeling and wondering how long we should stay. Here we were, five Mexican people sharing our crazy adventures with a swami, who was evidently more than busy, yet having a delightfully beautiful time. So I asked, "Shall we go now?" He said, "No!" We stayed for a while longer and agreed on times and dates for his visit to Mexico in the beginning of 2005.

When we left, we walked toward the white tall building where we were staying, planning to do a channeling session that Ame had requested. We could hear the musicians practicing for Amma's birthday celebration, chanting mantras, singing opera, and praying in French! There were Flamenco dancers, opera singers, The French Film association (who was recording the event to prepare a movie), Native American performers and artists, Tibetan dancers, Japanese artists, and many more. Such organization! People from all over the world were there: Europe, the United States, India, South America, and now Mexico.

That night Amma began singing *bhajans* in the main dining hall under crystal chandeliers. My mind stopped, my heart beat rapidly, and my ecstasy soared. Amma began chanting, and the devotion with which she sang was so powerful. I sang in response with all the others and again felt as if the room were empty. Sometimes I felt dizzy; sometimes just in a deeply pleasurable state. All the people were as intoxicating as Amma herself. How beautiful to be in the presence of so many souls singing, praying, chanting, and celebrating!

My friends, Govinda, Bhakti, and Deva had left the hall early. Deva had gone to call her family and meet new people. Govinda and Bhakti had gone back to their rooms. Deva would sometimes disappear and then come back telling us the most amazing stories. We were always asking, "Where is Leti, (Deva)?" But she was always creating a new experience for all of us and for herself.

When the *bhajans* came to completion after about an hour, I went to my room to try to get some rest. As soon as I arrived, I saw that Deva and Bhakti were almost asleep. I prepared myself to do the same when Ame came along. Feeling deeply emotional, I terribly missed my children, and I felt like quitting and going back to the safe world I knew! Ame acknowledged that we all felt like going back to Mexico to see our children. So, we should do it. "Family comes first," she said. Bhakti and Deva shared their longing for their children, too. Release happened for us, and we finally went to sleep. Ah! However, not before one more message from Ame to me, personally: "Ivonne will vomit all night long to cleanse and release whatever is not needed."

Impossible! I was not feeling sick. I had not eaten almost anything during the day, except for some curd, a *chapatti,* and a few sips of tea. Besides, I was taking healthy supplements to avoid bacteria and infections! Why would I be vomiting? I didn't even feel nauseated. I disregarded Ame's message and turned off the lights.

I closed my eyes to sleep and fifteen minutes later was rushing to the bathroom to empty my stomach. But my stomach was already empty! I vomited no food but something was coming up! I spent the whole night running into the bathroom. Finally, at 5 AM something shifted, and I was lucky to get two hours of profound and restful sleep.

In the morning, I related what had happened to my friends. We all wondered what could have upset my stomach. The night before at dinner, I had eaten something that I didn't feel like eating. Immersed in a mystical state, I had eaten three spoonfuls rather than one. But I had shared the exact meal with all my friends. They had eaten the same food! So what could it have been? Then I remembered that at lunch, a devotee of Amma's came to me and asked me if I would like Amma's *prasad*. I said, "Yes, of course," because in India, when a guru has leftovers from their meal, it is considered *prasad*, blessed food imbibed with the energy of the guru.

I ate the *prasad* from Amma, and my friends shared some, too. I had focused on the experience and prayed: *All food is a gift, may this gift deliver me whatever I need to purify and serve more completely.* Ha! Could it have been Amma's *prasad* that "aided" my purification? I choose to think it was!

We then had another session with Ame where she said, "Now that you all had your catharsis and release, let's continue with your creation in India." Her message immediately reminded me of a quote by Norman Vincent Peale:

*It's always too early to quit.*

# Darshan
## September 22

*Internal peace is an essential first step to achieving peace in the world.*
*How do you cultivate it? It's very simple. In the first place*
*by realizing clearly that all mankind is one, that human beings in every country*
*are members of one and the same family.*
*~ His Holiness the Dalai Lama*

The day evolved in the most peaceful way. Everyone on the ashram was preparing to leave to go to Cochin where Amma's birthday celebration was to be held. Buses were taking people at different times. We hired a private car to leave the following day. The mood on the ashram was sweet. Everyone was either packing or assisting in the packing. People were requesting assistance, and other people were walking by asking how they could be of service.

We had an appointment with the Ayurvedic doctor at the ashram. He had been with Amma for twenty years, and he told us, "Here I have become the richest man of all!" All of my friends and I had our pulses tested and our *doshas* (an Ayurvedic term for one's constitutional type) charted with this wonderful, meticulous doctor.

Suddenly a bell rang, which meant that Amma had spontaneously decided to give darshan. Her devotees and the people we met on the ashram all said the same thing, "Amma is an unexpected delight. She always asks us to be prepared for everything, but she never tells us what we will do or when." They also shared with us how all of them felt really close to their guru. The ashram has almost nine hundred permanent residents from all over the world. They all dress in white and look like angels. They all share amazing stories of their encounters with "the Mother," as they lovingly call her. They all express the same thing: They are very close to Amma, and they know everyone else is, too.

*Darshan* is a Sanskrit word meaning a vision of God. It is believed that through it you receive a divine blessing from an enlightened master, such as Amma, which contains *shaktipat* or healing energy through direct transmission. It is also believed that *darshan* facilitates the spiritual quest, accelerating the evolution of the Soul, removing Karma, purifying the body, mind, and spirit while raising the [1]*Kundalini* energy, creating balance in the chakras or energy vortexes in the human body.

In the few experiences that I have had regarding gurus, only once in a lifetime does someone get the chance to get close to the Master. While in the ashram,

Amma sometimes serves the food, or washes the septic tank, or calls one of her devotees in the middle of the night to teach her to sing in Spanish! She is a *Satguru*, yes, but mostly a beautiful human being who walks her talk and loves, and loves, and loves without ceasing. All of her devotees speak so beautifully of their relationship to Amma. I was deeply moved. Tears rolled silently down my face, my smile effortlessly grew, and my eyes slowly closed while I prayed, giving thanks for the energy I experienced.

When the *darshan* bell rang, we headed toward the temple. This time Bhakti and I decided to stay on the upper level, which was less crowded. Yet, when we looked down, we saw Deva sitting right in front of Amma's chair. How she managed to get so close, only she knows! The mood was one of grand expectation; people were whispering and wondering when and where Amma would appear this time. Many were already in lotus posture meditating, others arranging a blanket or pillows on the hard floor to sit comfortably. All of us were waiting for Amma when suddenly a young man named Satya announced, "I am sorry to inform you that one of the devotees thought Amma was coming to give *darshan*, but she is not. I am not going to tell you the name of this devotee." Everybody laughed. "Amma is busy preparing to go to Cochin tomorrow. I am sorry for any inconvenience this has caused all of you." With his smiley face, Satya went away, and I just couldn't do anything but laugh! What a great lesson of *expect the unexpected*. I was grateful for the moment and that Bhakti and I had decided to stay away from the crowds!

The afternoon was quiet. We did our official shopping for sandalwood malas, rose and jasmine incense, and different gifts. Then we went to the building where we were staying for we were to have another Ame session. I took the stairs instead of the elevator. My friends all followed and joined me in singing the *bhajans* that were running through my head. When we got to the 10th floor, a message came to me. Ame, my higher self, said, "Let's do the session on the beach. Go down the stairs again."

I gave the message to my friends, but we all decided first to go to our rooms to brush our teeth. As we reached our floor, we saw people running fast. One person

---

1.  Kundalini means 'coiled energy' and it refers to a power that lies in three-and-a-half coils in the sacrum bone called the Mooladhara, which is distinct from and lies above the Mooladhara Chakra. (It is interesting to note that *sacrum* is Greek for *sacred*.) A pulsation is sometimes seen at this level during Kundalini Awakening. Kundalini is normally in a potential state. When it is awakened, it ascends through the spine, across the void, to the top of the crown chakra. http://sahajayog.tripod.com/kundalini.htm

stopped and said, "Hurry! Amma has decided to give a *darshan* on the beach." Ha! There it was again—more validation in the moment. More *leelas* and more messages of: *There is no more time to lose, time is at hand.*

We walked to the beach. Amma was going to give *darshan* on the rooftop of the Ayurvedic clinic. When we arrived, Bhakti, Govinda, and Deva managed to get onto the roof. Akshmil and I stayed outside. It was really crowded; people seemed to be like sardines in a tin can. There was no space even to walk through anything or anyone and that was because many more people arrived from Europe for the celebration.

Amma sang and chanted, and then a message was announced, "Amma will be giving *darshan* only to the people that have just arrived today and haven't yet had *darshan* from her." I smiled because Akshmil and I were in the perfect place once again. We felt we received *darshan* from Amma anyway and, because we were outside and away from the crowd, we could easy walk back to the ashram.

We started back in the dark. The village was beautiful! Small houses made with coconut palm leaves, women in their colorful saris washing their clothes, the fragrance of people cooking in the village, the greeting smiles as we walked, the curiosity of children to see two strange Westerners dressed in white. While we walked, we shared our experiences. A woman asked us directions to the ashram. When we tried to explain, we found that we were lost! Ha! We had been walking and talking and, in the drunkenness of the moment, had not paid attention to where we were going.

The woman who had asked us for assistance was actually the one who helped us find our way back. What a message from the universe! Isn't life itself the most sublime message of the Divine?

# To Cochin
## September 23

*The whole world we travel with our thoughts,*
*Finding nowhere anyone as precious as one's own self.*
*Since each and every person is so precious to themselves*
*Let the self-respecting harm no other being.*
*~ Samyutta Nikaya*

We awoke the next day and I already felt the butterflies of anticipation of our next adventure. At the same time, I felt a longing and gratitude toward all the residents and the energy of the ashram itself. At 10:30 that morning, we headed toward Cochin.

Our drive out of Kerala was the exact opposite from our arrival. It was daytime now, and our driver was relaxed, taking his time. He was not in a rush at all. The views of the countryside were beautiful. In the ocean there were many fishermen preparing their boats and equipment to go fishing. White birds shared their flight with our eyes, and people were already walking, carrying candles for the morning prayers. I slept a while and, when I woke, I watched in bewilderment the beauty of a seaside village. There were a few small houses in the center of the village. There was a small temple built with adobe and the roof had a stature of Lord Vishnu, who people believe is the guardian of the village. Children and elders sat on the floor while the priests passed a fire to bless all. I contemplated the simplicity of it all. I was in India, but beauty can be found everywhere. You don't need to travel to see a sunset. Wherever you are, and no matter the language that you speak, or how much money you have in your pocket, the sun will surely come out and share its golden rays.

After three-and-a-half hours, we arrived at Cochin. The energy was much more intense here. There were many huge banners welcoming people from all over the world to the birthday celebration of Amma sponsored by different corporations and spiritual organizations from all over the world. Different ads from corporations bestowed their *pranams,* their respect, to Amma. Cochin was full of these welcoming messages and full of little motorcycle rickshaws, a motorcycle inside a little cabin that serves as a taxi and that abounds in India.

We took Bhakti and Govinda to the Wytefort Hotel, and then Deva, Akshmil, and I arrived at Le Meridien Hotel. I must say, the comfort was like being in heaven! After an ashram, the opulence was very tempting. Although Amma's ashram offered superb conditions for us, Le Meridien's softness looked very nice indeed. We were received with a *Namaste* and offered coconut-lime water to drink. Our bags were taken care of and everything was perfect. Yet, I began noticing in my mind a hint of doubt for no matter what the place looked like and no matter where I was; the real pleasure, the real comfort and luxury, resided in my heart.

I began to admire a certain detachment from material things and an enjoyment of them as well. At the same time, I saw within myself a longing to live in a simple way. While thinking those things, I decided to enjoy the manifestation of comfort. My friends and I went to the Ayurvedic Spa in the hotel where we received their heavenly treatments!

Every day for the next five days we would delight in the Ayurvedic world and the pleasure of massage given by two people at the same time. That night we had dinner, then a session with Ame, and then to sleep.

# Embracing the World
## The Celebration Begins
## September 24–27

There is one Truth that shines through all of Creation.
Rivers and mountains, plants and animals, the sun, the moon, and the stars,
you and I, all are expressions of this one reality.
*~ Sri Mata Amritanandamayi Devi*

We planned our days based on our Ayurvedic appointments. In downtown Cochin—which reminded me of Mexico with small clothes stores and grocery shops surrounded by temples, ocean, and different people—at a huge sports stadium, Amma's birthday celebration would be taking place for four days. There would be art performances, talks by different religious leaders of the world, workshops by corporate business associates, presentations by women devotees, exhibitions, free food—everything!

However, we had just arrived, and we definitely wanted to explore the city. We reviewed the calendar of events and decided to attend only the inauguration ceremony where Amma would be present with the Deputy Prime Minister of India, L. K. Advani, other government officials, and well-known personalities.

We took a fantastic trip in a big boat around the green wide lagoon, called Backwaters (also know as the Chambacara Channel). We sat on the upper level with only a batik-style cloth with rainbow colors as a roof protecting us from the sun's rays. We embarked on a two-hour journey in silence (Ame's advice) to observe the wonders and the stillness of the fishermen, which seemed motionless, the village, and the magic of the water itself.

The fishermen were seemingly alone in their little boats. I contemplated the meditative experience that their life was for them—they needed to be very attentive to catch the fish; they had no distractions, and they, too, were silent. On our way, we were delighted to see a whitetail hawk fly by more than once. The sounds of the water and now and then the motors of the boats added to my contemplation.

The beautiful village people ran down to the shore just to wave at us. Children with their tilak marks and Indian clothes smiled at us as a song of love. Some of them practiced their English by saying hello, while others delighted in watching these strangers from another country wave back at them. I fell into a deep state of silence the more I observed. I had my eyes open all the time. Usually, when I must observe silence (during my Yoga classes or in meditation), I close my eyes.

I have a very talkative personality, but somehow the focus, the energy, and the altered state of consciousness I was experiencing delivered a quietude inside and outside of me that was a renewal and easy to pursue and enjoy. I felt the power of silence for the first time. It was deep, a moment where my mind created no thoughts. It was not only to be quiet with the voice, but also to feel and experience the quiet language of the Divine. That allowed me to discover beautiful things that usually, when I am talking, I miss.

There were white and yellow lilies in the water, and gentle waves created by the boats. The whitetail hawk flew overhead again. A white small butterfly landed on a flower. I delighted in watching my friends observe their silences, too.

We took some pictures, and my camera got wet. I really didn't care that all the film was spoiled. I was internally laughing at myself because this was my creation as well. Before going to India, I told my Yoga teacher that I would not be taking any pictures. I had decided that taking care of a camera might be distracting. I simply wanted to "film my trip" with my heart and memory. Of course, as soon as I got to India, I wanted to take pictures! Here I was in the beautiful Backwaters with my spoiled film manifesting from my own intention. I was smiling because what else was there to do? Besides, my friends had cameras and were taking wonderful pictures.

Exactly an hour and a half into our trip, I heard a deep and loud voice saying, "Look for me." I don't recall all the details, but suddenly and spontaneously the name *"Babaji"* began to vibrate louder in my head. I watched my thoughts, and this time I closed my eyes and saw his figure. When I opened my eyes, I perceived a particular alertness and experienced someone calling to me.

On my right, I saw a small field of green grass. There were no structures, no one there, just grass floating as a little tiny island in the lagoon. When I looked, it was lovely and empty, just grass. On the left, there were children from the village waving to us. I waved back, and suddenly I felt drawn to look to the right again. Now the view was different. The grassy spot that seemed empty before now had a man sitting in the lotus position, black long hair in a ponytail, dressed in white with a huge smile on his face! He was waving at Alex and me.

Then he did something that got my attention, and I noticed that Alex's attention was caught by it, too. He was moving his arms in a circular motion, signaling his right eye, and then pointing at us saying, "I'll see you later!" Then he said something else in English. The energy I felt was intense. A tingling cold and warm sensation ran through my spine. I focused and thanked him, and he responded with *Namaste* and created with his hands the movement of a number eight figure. He bowed at us, and our boat continued. After a couple of moments,

I tried looking back to see the man, but no one was there. My mind repeated only one name: *Babaji, Babaji, and Babaji.* Later, Alex told me that he had experienced the same thing at the same time while in the boat.

We arrived at the hotel in stillness and silence, took a picture, and then began our talking communication again. After two hours of observing silence, it was difficult for me to speak as I usually did—rapidly and without much thought to what I am saying. This time, I observed each word that I wanted to say to make sure that it would contribute with love and joy rather than just as noise to "fill the space."

We headed toward an amazing banquet of truly remarkable food. I ate a whole dish of *paneer*, Indian cottage cheese with spinach, with a *chapatti* and *curd*, some sweet *lassi masala* yogurt beverage, and a wonderful carrot and cardamom cake. I was still getting "high" from eating but noticed that "eating air" was actually beginning to be a normal part of the experience. Air filled me like food, and I spontaneously tried to chew it.

When the time came to go to the stadium for the Celebration Inauguration, I went to arrange a private car for our transportation. I saw a young American man, Andrew (whose spiritual name given by Amma is *Nirag* which means dispelling darkness), whom I recognized from the *darshan* with Amma. I felt drawn to invite him to come with us.

Funny, wise, and sharp, Andrew delighted us with his experiences as a doctor, as an interfaith minister, and as a devotee of Amma's. While in the car, I decided to give him one of my books, *The Soul mate Called God*. Andrew was very grateful, and I experienced a sensation that I had found an old friend or a brother.

We arrive at the stadium, and we were amazed at the thousands of people there. It seemed like the Super Bowl for me! Guards, flags from all over the world, people speaking in different languages. The newspapers later reported that more than a million people were in attendance.

We did not know where to go but, as always, we trusted and were divinely guided. I felt a hunch to go in a certain direction, and our guide and angel, Gautam, manifested for us with his usual smile and pleasure to serve! He immediately took us to the entrance and secured places for us close to the stage. We were given the V. D. T status: *Very Divine Treatment.*

All throughout our time in India, we were always assisted in divine ways. Everything was always on time. The right person met us at the right place. We were always more than comfortable with great seats and beautiful, courteous people helping us. There was magic, magic, and more magic everywhere we went!

When the inauguration started, the Deputy Prime Minister of India, L. K. Advani, along with many other dignitaries, addressed the audience and offered flower garlands to Amma. How spiritual the energy of the Deputy Prime Minister was. He very carefully, with his heart, selected each word of his speech. Alex and I especially were deeply touched. Throughout all the speeches, Andrew was trying to translate the words into Spanish for my friends, although he mostly spoke Italian. After a while, we just decided to hear the native words themselves.

We arrived back at the hotel two hours later for our Ayurvedic treatment, and I swear I entered heaven. I was treated to a massage called *Abhvangam*. Two beautiful girls worked lukewarm herbal oil into my head and body, which is the traditional Kerala-style. The energy was beautiful, professional, and healing. I felt honored, respected, and well cared for.

That night during dinner, two Indian women sang. They had such wonderful voices. Just as I was wishing they would sing one of my favorite songs, "Love is in the Air," they began to sing it! This song has become the official hymn of all the workshops we have given. It is always a celebratory song where we dance and delight in the blessings of love. In silence, I gave thanks for the manifestation. After dinner we had a channeling session with Ame, with our beloved friend Andrew as a guest. Then we went to sleep.

Over the next few days, our attention was diverted by shopping in the local markets and sightseeing. We visited the Raj Palace and were told about the stories painted on the walls and ceilings of Vishnu disguising himself as a woman to seduce Shiva to experience Divine Love with a God. As I listened to the story, I had vivid visions of Vishnu and Shiva making love, and my heart felt opened with love and respect for sexual energy as a sacred portal of the Divine. We then visited the St. Francis temple, a traditional Catholic temple built in the year 1499. I felt a peaceful and silent environment. Usually, in all the temples in India, music is playing or a loud something is going on. The temples are often crowded with devotees, yet this one was empty and quiet. It is actually the temple that [2]Vasco de Gama found and in which he was first buried before his body was removed to Portugal, the country of his birth.

We meditated for a while and, when I closed my eyes, I perceived the fragrance of sandalwood and roses. I opened my eyes thinking that perhaps someone

2.   Vasco de Gama is famous for his completion of the first all-water trade route between Europe and India. Vasco de Gama finally arrived in Calicut, India on May 20, 1498. He died on December 24, 1524. Vasco de Gama's remains were taken back to Portugal, where he was buried in the chapel where he had prayed before his first voyage. http://campus.northpark.edu/history/WebChron/WestEurope/DaGama.html

sat next to me that was wearing an exquisite perfume, but, of course, no one was there and yet the fragrance continued to permeate the air with its presence. We walked slowly out of the temple, and I vowed to the Creator for the diversity in the unity that awe all are, in beliefs, temples, and fragrances!

We visited the spice market. The fragrance was captivating. Ginger, cardamom, clove, and saffron seasoned the air and our eyes with their tasty colors. In the brass market, I found an antique ring made out of different stones that represented the planets in the shape of a peacock. It looked like [3]Parvati (Shiva's Shakti or Soul mate). It fit my finger perfectly, and I was pleased to have found that treasure, so I bought it. As soon I put it in my finger a vision came: A majestic white peacock looked at me and transformed into a beautiful woman with dark long hair and deep brown eyes. The vision was interrupted as a young man came to offer me to buy a carpet.

The Kashmiri storeowners had an amazing persuasive skill that could entice you to buy almost anything, whether you could afford it or not. The son of the owner of one of the stores, a young man with beautiful big brown eyes, had been assisting us and flattered me every time he could. One day, as his father was trying to sell me some really expensive things that I did not want to buy, I said, "If I buy this, my husband might divorce me!" The young man replied, "Good! Then I can marry you."

So in between shopping, laughing with Andrew, channeling with Ame, visiting temples, and being pampered by the most amazing Ayurvedic doctors, we experienced Cochin as the most beautiful, relaxing, and entertaining time so far, but the best was yet to come!

---

3.    Parvati, a Hindu goddess. In her it is said that we can have the true celebration of Hindu womanhood. Of unsurpassed sensual beauty, her endowment is not merely physical but spiritual, not narcissistic but meant as an offering. In her it can be said that we have the grand personification of the Hindu expression, as well as the concept of beauty. In classical mythology, the raison of Parvati's birth is to lure Shiva into marriage. http://www.exoticindia.com/article/parvati

# The Convergence of Waters
## Jala Maha Sangamam
## September 26

Peace be to earth and to airy spaces!
Peace be to heaven, peace be to the waters!
Peace to the plants and peace to the trees!
May all the Gods grant to me peace!
By this invocation of peace may peace be diffused!
~ *Atharva Veda*

With Friday came time to participate in the *Jala Jala Maha Sangamam Ceremony*—The Convergence of Waters—as the representatives of Mexico. It was during the *Amritavarsham 50th* (birthday celebration), and many countries in the world participated. Holy water from all the participating nations, from the 191 member countries of the United Nations, and from the seven sacred rivers of India were brought to the venue of the celebration. We brought water from both the ocean of Cancun and [4] *Tlacote* water—well known in Mexico for its remarkable healing properties. Scientists studied it and discovered that the water has intelligent microorganisms that reproduce themselves to create healing.

A wonderful procession took place both inside and outside of the Jawaharlal Nehru International Stadium. All the representatives of the countries lined up dressed in the traditional costume of the country they represented. Smiling, prying, chanting, and crying, we all were overwhelmed in joy of witnessing and participating in such a memorable moment, all as one.

I had the honor of carrying the water, Alex carried the Mexican flag, and Bhakti held a lit candle. The ceremony's intention was world peace.

As we were walking, I thought that I had always dreamed about participating in the Olympic Games when I was little. Here I was in a procession with participants from many countries, but this had gone beyond my expectations. All the people were singing one mantra:

[5]LOKAH

SAMASTAH

---

4.  Tlacote healing water emanates from the soil at Queretaro, Mexico.
5.  The meaning of this mantra is: May all beings live in peace and happiness.

SUKHINO

BHAVANTU

The reverberation of the chant was the most amazing lullaby. All of us were dressed in the traditional costumes from the countries we represented, but, of course, we decided to create our own version of the traditional Mexican outfit. We were dressed in white with Mexican handmade embroidered shirts, Mexican "sombreros," and "Viva México" spirit. I was carrying an image of the Virgin of Guadalupe on a cloth bag that held the water from our country.

As soon as I walked inside the big round stadium, I noticed that my bag was turned by the wind and the image of the Virgin was facing straight ahead toward the waiting crowds. I felt a warm, nurturing energy. I felt shivers once again from the tip of my toes to the top of my head. I knew that the presence of the holy Mother was there. I felt her and acknowledged internally her sacred presence.

We were greeted by many people when they saw our Mexican flag. They shouted, "MEXICO!" I never thought that I would feel such pride for my country. I mean, we all are part of the same world. What difference does it make if one is born here or there? Aren't our destinies the same no matter where we are from? The search for and the Divine Understanding of who we are as Love, as Source and God happens wherever we live. Yet, I did feel a joy and an amazing gratitude toward Mexico and its mysticism and the presence of the holy Mother of Guadalupe—the Beloved of all Mexicans.

The sun was really hot that day. At the end of the procession, two swamis collected the water from each country and poured it into one big vessel, which was then offered first to Amma, who blessed it. Then it was presented to the President of India, A. P. J. Abdul Kalam, and poured at the root of a kalpaturu tree sapling (a banyan sapling representative of the legendary "*Kalpatharu Vriksham*," the "Wish Fulfilling Tree"). It was a moving moment—chanting, the waving of flags, thousands of people, dignitaries, swamis, children—all in the midst of a grand celebration. Tears of joy were pouring from every person I looked at.

Bhakti still carried the candle representing the light of Mexico. After a few minutes, a swami came to us, holding in his hands a beautiful picture of Amma with her hands in *Namaste*. He took the candle from Bhakti, and it seemed that Amma was the one taking it—a beautiful sign.

The President of India then addressed all the people, calling upon the youth to make India economically strong with an integrated spiritual life if they wished to live in a peaceful, prosperous, and safe country. I immediately prayed and wished for all presidents in all countries and their people to have an integrated spiritual life and demonstrate their request. Mr. Kalam then asked the young people to dream and question everything with a scientific temperament for achieving greatness.

He continued:

> *Love whatever profession you might journey in your life.*
> *Teach at least ten people to read and write.*
> *Plant at least ten saplings and ensure their growth.*
> *Go to both rural and urban areas and help at least five people to free themselves from addictions.*
> *Be responsible in removing the pain of ailing people.*
> *Do not support any differentiation in community or language.*
> *Live an honest life free from corruption.*
> *Set an example and lead a transparent life.*
> *Be a friend of the mentally and physically challenged and celebrate the success of the country and its people.*

In the stadium, however, I was filled with an overwhelming energy. My mind had "too many things to do" thoughts. My focus was in not spilling the water I was carrying. My mind was telling me, "It's time to leave. You have an Ayurvedic appointment." Being so "busy," I just couldn't really understand the President's message, but now that I have rewritten it, I realize just how powerful it is. Wouldn't it be great for all countries if we really practiced at least two of those things?

It all comes down to one word: Love!

That night I had the most real dream. I was arriving at an ashram, which happened to be Satya Sai Baba's. He personally received me with two bodyguards. I smiled at him, and he telepathically said to me, "You cannot come in!" In my dream I was astonished and replied, "What do you mean? We are from Mexico!" Then Sai Baba contemplated that, smiled, and said, "Welcome." The dream shifted, and I found myself in the midst of a big audience waiting for him to give *darshan*. Huge high-tech TVs in the sky showed Sai Baba creating his miracles and giving his blessings. The vibe in my dream was like a superstar rock concert. I said to myself, I will be just watching. In the morning when I woke up, I told my roommate, Leti, about my vivid dream, and she said, "I dreamt about Sai Baba, too, last night." A *leela* once again!

Later on that same day, sitting in the lobby with my friend Alex, I noticed a book with the picture of Sai Baba on a shelf. Pulled toward it, I requested permission from a man who was cleaning the room to have a look. The cover had a huge picture of Sai Baba on it. On the first page was a letter signed by Sai Baba to the author. I entered into an altered state in which I felt the letter was directed to me. I tried to shift this, thinking that it must just be my imagination. But I couldn't. The energy was very strong. I read the letter. "Welcome back," Sai Baba had written. "I've been waiting so long for you. Your journey is one of magic, and you should pursue your dreams. Many voices will raise their beliefs against you or in favor of you, but you shall always follow your heart."

This message was perfect for me. While wondering about our visit to Puttaparthi, I was having second thoughts about going, so I took this as a confirmation that we should go to Sai Baba's ashram. I returned the book, which was dedicated to the hotel where we were staying. Hours later, when I wanted to show the book to some of my friends, it was gone. I asked the waiter, but he said he didn't know anything about it. I didn't remember the face of the cleaning man, but it was not important anymore. I had gotten the message loud and clear.

Inside the stadium where the celebration EMBRACE THE WORLD took place and the Convergence of Waters united all countries, religions, and belief systems for one day with the intention of unity, love, and peace. © Mastery Life A.C

# Happy Birthday!

*True innocence is pure love endowed with discrimination and understanding.*
*~ Sri Mata Amritanandamayi Devi*

The twenty-seventh had finally arrived! Amma's birthday! We were going to assist early in the morning, but we decided to behave and follow the rules this time. (We had obviously skipped the whole Cochin program over the past week.) We took the special bus that the Ammachi Organization had prepared for all the attendees, and we headed toward the stadium, singing *bhajans*, laughing, watching the craziness of the traffic, and feeling a deep ecstatic mood of celebration!

When we arrived, we were met by Beloved Gautam. All the people assisting were very tired, but the blissful smiles on their faces were constant. They were high from the overwhelming experience of joy and of serving people from all over the world. After a week of solving problems of transportation, stolen passports, and giving endless directions, they were still always willing to serve. We felt drawn to assist them. Leti gave massages to many of the women there. Alex did, too, to the men. It was the least we could do to serve them. Their work was extraordinary—no complaints—just joy and pure service!

Then the time came when Gautam asked us to come with him to receive *darshan* from Amma. She was marrying 108 couples who didn't have money to marry on their own. In India, wedding celebrations are very expensive. Amma married them for free, with her blessing. She announced to the entire stadium that she would be there all day and night until the last person could meet with her and have her *darshan*!

Thanks to our VDT status and with the help of Gautam, he led us toward a podium where Amma was sitting. Amma's eyes were the pure intoxication of love. I could see like a rainbow fountain of love pouring through her eyes. She was high in the ecstasy of service. Her devotees had so much hope and faith, hugging her with so much love. Don't you think you would get drunk with that, too? Isn't the grandest joy to be able to see the smiles and openness of the hearts of other fellow human beings?

My turn came and, once again, Amma pulled me strongly toward her. This time she spoke to me in Spanish saying, "*Hija mia, hija mia.*" (Daughter of mine. Daughter of mine.) During her hug, my thoughts were, "I love you for the work you do and for the manifestation you have accomplished. May God bless you with health and more joy." For *prasad*, she gave me a delicious *laddu* candy, a small ball of flour sautéed in cashew nuts, raisins, and sugar that is known to be the favorite of Lord Ganesha. I ate it and immediately got dizzy, literally, but from what? Amma's energy? My energy? The thousands of people in the stadium waiting for her?

The sensation emptied my mind once again. I sat very close to her, watching with amusement her amazing energy. Amma gave each person different messages, different gifts of *prasad*, but always with the same warm embrace and the same huge smile.

Then Leti began assisting her in giving out *prasad* to all the people! She had just had Amma's *darshan* and there she was, once again right up front. How did she do it? The Leti Mystery will remain forever. Security was intense, yet Leti always managed to get close to all of the gurus, demonstrating very useful Mexican skills. It was such a delight to see her. Her pure intention manifested that reality.

As I was sitting close by Amma, just watching, I felt drawn to look over to my right, and a strong, loving energy came shoulder to shoulder with me. I saw a beautiful monk from Japan dressed in red with his bold hair and shining smile. He did not speak English or Spanish, and I did not speak Japanese. But still we had a strong connection. He asked for my e-mail, I gave him my Web site, and he invited me to visit Japan. Gautam saw that I was speaking with him, or at least trying to. Later Gautam told me that this monk was one of the most important religious authorities in Japan. And there he was bowing to Amma and receiving her *darshan* like everybody else.

A beautiful swami came by and asked me to move to the side where the women were sitting. He was so kind; I took from my wrist an amber mala and gave it to him. I just felt drawn to do that. He kissed it, and I was so happy to see him smiling! He was such a delight. He must have been at least seventy years old with a skinny body and a long white beard.

As I walked to the women's side where Amma's assistants were sitting, I witnessed my mind to be very quiet...no thoughts at all. I tried to put some thoughts into it, but the more I tried, the more I couldn't find any thoughts. I attempted to articulate language and to speak with a woman close to me, but the words wouldn't come from my mind. Then in a deep state of bliss, I managed to ask, "Amma, is this really happening?" Suddenly, she turned toward me and looked at me. With a glance like all the deities have (I swear I saw all deities through her at that instant!), she nodded to me.

After the *darshan*, we all went back to Gautam's to say farewell. We didn't want to leave. We were in love with him and with Amma and both the extraordinary and ordinary experiences at the ashram. The romance with existence continued. We wanted to hug Gautam and his friends, but the traditional customs would not allow it. It was ironic; however, that Amma's way of blessing people—children, men, women of all races and ages—was by hugging. Instead, I visualized the hug and then with longing and readiness for the next adventure, we headed back to our hotel.

On the way out, a young man approached me and asked if I would be willing to be interviewed for TV. I agreed and included Alex in this experience with me. We were asked some questions, and I played with a few of the children that were there.

Back at the hotel, Alex and I went to the restaurant for some *lassi* and dessert. There we met two disciples of Amma's from the USA. They were not only a delight to visit with, but also were very interested in how we got there. They had been longtime disciples of Amma. She had even stayed once in their home. They were honored to share their story with us. Their given names were Satya and Suchindra. They told us they heard us singing *bhajans* and were curious as to how we had learned them so fast. In just a few moments, we were all sharing experiences and the energy of recognition. We talked of gurus from Muktananda to Amma. I had a beautiful time with them. I wished for them to remain in the light that they were demonstrating and for them to be happy.

The time came for our last Ayurvedic treatment. I had the good fortune to experience *Dhara*, a process developed in Kerala. A steady steam of medicated oil or buttermilk is poured on the head, especially on the forehead, in a particular pattern. It is a massage for mental relaxation and heightened meditative experiences. It was divine. I was tired and walking very slowly, feeling empty, in a good way, like a baby. Ahhhhh, such a sweet sensation. It was perfect to have the *Dhara* the night before we were to begin traveling again. I said farewell to my new friends who had been massaging me for the last five days. I gave them some gifts and received back the gift of their smiling eyes.

All of us headed toward the dining room with Andrew, Alex, and the young Ayurvedic doctor. He took me aside and told me, "You are a problem reliever! You have a lot of *satya!* (spiritual energy) Your pulse is strong; I can tell from your dosha." I tried to understand the meaning of this, but it is still not very clear to me. The only thing I secretly wished for was that my husband would hear him say that I was a problem reliever instead of a problem giver! Ha!

# 3

## *Masculine Energy*

You are the creator and destroyer and our protector.
You shine as the sun in the sky;
You are the source of all light.
When you pour yourself down as rain on earth,
Every living creature is filled with joy
And knows food will be abundant for all.

~ *Prashna Upanishad*

# The Magic of Bangalore
## September 28

*Create, manifest, dissolve, and merge within the Ganges of Divine wisdom,*
*kissing thy Shakti inside the heart*
*and dancing the everlasting song of eternal cycles.*
*~ Ivonne Delaflor*

Andrew came with us to the airport. The car was full of bags. They were increasing in number as the days went by. Our flight to Bangalore was delayed, but Andrew's flight to Delhi was on time. We all gathered for breakfast before he left. I drank a *lassi,* and my friends ate some pancakes and eggs. Saying *hasta luego* to Andrew was very moving. By now he felt like a brother to us. I had experienced so much love and nurturing being with him. His blue eyes were sparkling. We all hugged, and he expressed how nice it had been for him to meet us. It was a reflection of our feelings, too.

During the flight to Bangalore, I held one question in my mind, "Where shall we go first?" Then I remembered I was carrying the book, *The Initiation,* and randomly selected a page. Of course, I opened exactly to the place where Prema Baba was in Bangalore, and he was being taken to a Shiva Temple. In front of a huge Shiva, he wished for wealth and happiness for his family.

I took this as Divine direction. As soon as we arrived in Bangalore, I told our driver that the first thing I wanted to do was to go to the nearest Shiva temple. He took us to a place that looked more like a shopping center, and I was not at all interested in shopping. I only wanted to meet Shiva and to be in the temple and mediate. But he told us to walk around the alley and there would be a temple. I thought it might be a small temple but, of course, things are not usually what they seem. When we arrived, we left our shoes outside and gave a donation for an offering of sweet milk to be used in our puja. We were invited to perform a ritual where we poured some of the sweet milk onto a *lingam* (an egg-shaped stone symbolic of the Divine Masculine, considered to be the actual form of Shiva in the world) at the entrance.

I asked one of the *pujaris* (an attendant who offers puja) if he could guide us through the temple. When we came to the center that was open to the sky, we were greeted by a huge statue of Lord Shiva that was three-stories high and constructed of what seemed to be white marble, with two big brown mala necklaces around his neck and two cobras by each of his arms. I was amazed and delighted. The *pujari* then took us to the altar of Shiva lingams and explained their meaning. We went through a dark hall that smelled like mold. There we saw the different lingams built in crystal, ice, gold, copper, and wood, all illuminated with candles. Each represented the diverse powers of Lord Shiva, from warrior to sensual master. The *pujari* shared each story with grand honor as if Lord Shiva was really present, and I think he was. Then the *pujari* performed a puja, and we received sacred food and drink that was offered first to the deity.

At the end of the guided Shiva tour, we came to a pond in front of the Shiva statue. You could stand in front of the Lord, make a wish, and throw in a special golden coin from the temple. When it was my turn to make my wish and throw the coin, I took a little time to think about it. I have been so blessed in my life! I know that my family will always be taken care of. Source, Existence itself, will always make sure that they experience the most sacred things for their evolution. I know my friends are going to be well. What could I wish for? Then it came to me. "I wish for God as Existence, as Divine Source, to grant all the wishes of all the people that with a pure intention and open heart petition God. I wish for Prema Baba's wish to be fulfilled." Then, just like writing a letter to Santa Claus, I continued. "I wish for peace in the world, for Mother Earth to be healthy, for people to love and not be afraid to do so, and for me to be reminded of humbleness each time I forget." I closed my eyes and with all my faith and innocence, I threw the coin into the water.

What a happy moment!

I went back to the small temple to the statues of the deities. People were circumambulating them three times. I decided to do it nine times, and I suggested to my friends to do the same. As we went round and round, Bhakti was approached by a *pujari,* telling her that only three rounds were necessary. Oops…were we breaking the rules again? Or perhaps just creating a new moment of joy?

After that, we were taken to the Bangalore Gardens. The most ancient stone in the world is found there. We were met with beautiful, friendly trees, from banyans to rudrashka trees, and trees from all over the world. We sat for a while in the large and sweeping branches of a huge banyan tree to meditate. Then the gardener offered to sell us some seeds—lotus, jasmine, sandalwood, and banyan tree seeds.

As we were heading back to the entrance to the botanical gardens, a couple of people approached us and were drawn to my friend Alex. They spontaneously called him Swamiji and requested his blessings. Alex's response was of surprise and humbleness. His eyes looked like those of a child who looks at his Mother for a possible explanation regarding a new situation. It was a delight to watch. And it is such a responsibility when someone trusts in you. A devotee with a teacher is much like a child with his parents.

We were taken to a very nice upscale restaurant for lunch. The art on the walls depicted royalty. The architecture was different from that in Kerala, too. There were many white domes and engraved stones on the walls creating flower shapes. It was beautiful. The meal was supreme. The manager took care of us once again. I told him we would trust him with his selections, and he delivered dish after dish of succulent Indian food. We did have a request though: NOT SPICY, PLEASE. Many times the spices in the food were so strong that even our Mexican *picante* couldn't take it. For the first time during our trip, we ordered a bottle of wine. As I was drinking it, I quickly became drunk in love again. A relaxing energy filled my stomach that felt like I was being hugged by existence at all times.

Afterward, we met with our driver who took us to our last Bangalore destination, the ISKON temple. What an adventure that was! Silently, I begged that my friends not stop for any shopping distractions, which was contrary to the intention of our trip. Lessons would arise about that in the days to come. It was very clear for all of us in regard to the choices we made and the consequences we manifested.

Swami Amenanda & Swami Akshmilanandaji (a very psychic person and disciple of Maharishi whose connection with angels and subtle dimensions have served many people to regain their path of love, has published three books and recorded two devotional CDs) at the Shiva Temple in Bangalore. © Mastery Life A.C

# The ISKON Temple

The ISKON temple in Bangalore is one of the largest Krishna temples in India. The architecture is a combination of traditional Karnataka and modern styles to give it aesthetic style as well as the best of the latest scientific technology. As you enter the main temple, it leads you to the main hall, which is 9,000 square feet with a free span of 100 feet by 60 feet high, where around two thousand people can take *darshan* at a time. The main altars have three gold-plated ceilings. The main deities are made of five different metals and are gold-plated. The temple hall also has six galleries with forty windows. There are three main entrances to the temple hall facing north, east, and west. All around the temple is an inner passage, then an outer passage for the movement of the Krishna energy during festival times. Honestly, the architecture was exquisite. It was a very modern facility and, with all due respect to my materialistic thoughts, it looked more like a shopping center than a temple.

The temple was built to honor Lord Krishna and his devotees.

Sri Madhu Pandit Dasa, the President & Project Director, ISKON, Bangalore, says:

*"The ISKON temple provides much more for the soul than those rituals. ISKON temples are centers of spiritual learning through godly association, centers where a visitor is inspired to learn about spiritual life. One can receive practical guidance in his spiritual life from those who are already on the path of spiritual advancement. Although the senses of the visitors may be bogged down by absorption in material endeavor, they can be purified and enlivened by coming in touch with the Supreme Lord in various ways and experience happiness. This temple provides such transcendental experiences as seeing the beautiful form of the Lord and participating in hearing and singing. Thus, step-by-step, they will realize the reality of their own spiritual identity and learn to cater to its needs."*

Thousands of people were there that day. I was a little bit concerned about time because we had to meet a friend in Puttaparthi at Sai Baba's ashram to arrange our stay. The drive from Bangalore to Puttaparthi was four hours, and it was getting late. A specific protocol had to be followed to be able to enter the temple. My impetuous nature saw a shortcut, and I began to head that way. A *pujari* called after me, "Please madam, not that way!" But I continued and, with Leti, we quickly arrived at the main shrine. My other friends followed the whole Krishna protocol that involved climbing many stairs, skipping stones, chanting the name of Krishna, ringing bells, and so on, which was actually a good experience for them.

The celebration of [1]Navaratri started the same day we arrived in Bangalore. Thousands of people were in the streets celebrating and praying. The Krishna temple was really crowded! It was so hard to even walk.

On our way out, a *pujari* chose Leti and me from the whole crowd to have his Arati blessing. He offered us *agni* (the sacred fire), tilak (sacred ashes) for our foreheads, and *prasad* of sweet rice. I tried to relax, but the butterflies in my stomach were flying stronger. I had a sensation that my mind couldn't explain regarding Puttaparthi, however, I disregarded it for the moment. Before we left the temple, I bought a CD-ROM of the *Bhagavad-Gita* for my children. Yes, I was shopping again! It took a few minutes to gather everyone together at the car and to find the driver, but soon we were headed toward Puttaparthi.

---

1.   Navaratri is a festival that lasts nine days and nine nights. The word Navaratri actually means nine (Nava) nights (ratri). The most significant part of Navaratri is the setting up an odd number of steps (usually seven, nine, or eleven) and the placement of different idols of gods on them. Navaratri is the worship of the three divine goddesses, Saraswati (goddess of learning and speech), Lakshmi (goddess of wealth and prosperity), and Durga (goddess of strength and courage). It is also said to be the battle that occurred between Goddess Chaamundeshwari and the asura (demon), Mahishaasura. The battle lasted nine days and nine nights. Finally, on the tenth day, Goddess Chaamundeshwari killed Mahishaasura. This day is known as Vijayadasami. Vijayadasami means the tenth day of victory. http://www.carnatic.com/karmasaya/index.php?Navaratri

# Om Sri Sai Ram

*If you see me, I see you.*
*~ Satya Sai Baba*

Our journey took longer than expected. My mind was intently focused on getting to Puttaparthi. On the way, the beautiful scenery accompanied us with a new fragrance of dusty air and a different vibration—rock formations, mountains, gorgeous trees, and nearly empty roads. We stopped several times for the driver to pay taxes, or something like that. Each time he stopped, many people came close to the windows, trying to sell us things or begging for money. We were previously warned not give anything to anyone because we would then have the whole town in front of us, begging in our faces. It was very hard for me to ignore the beggars and to be firm in saying "no." It was especially hard when children were asking for money. My heart contracted each time.

On one occasion, I decided to give something to the next person who requested it. But suddenly in my mind I could hear my Yoga teacher's (Bhavani's) voice, saying to me, "Remember that one of the principles of Yoga is not to steal opportunities from people!" Then she offered the example of people who could have a decent job but who chose to be beggars instead. Sometimes it was easier for them to just beg. By assisting them, it may be stealing from them the opportunity to evolve into something better. But I disregarded the message and, instead of money, I gave away some pens.

We arrived at a crossing that divided two small villages, and the train was passing by. We were very close to Puttaparthi now, but the four-hour drive had turned into five hours. The driver told us that he needed to ask directions. Everywhere were pictures of Sai Baba—everywhere. All the cars had the words *Jai Ram* written on them, the greeting they would all give honoring the Avatar.

My temper readied to flare. The feeling had more of a Yang quality rather than my nurturing feminine Yin energy that I had been feeling since my arrival in India. Something different was definitely happening. The "doer" energy, the "accomplisher" energy, arose. I could feel it everywhere—in the faces of the people, in the way they moved. I could feel it inside my mind—with sudden emotional coldness.

We finally arrived in Puttaparthi and crossed the Ganesha Gate, a structure built as the entrance to what I called "The Sai Ram World." Built as an arch, it had a statue of Lord Ganesha as the welcoming deity to this unknown world. The whole city was planned and developed by Sai Baba. The well-defined roads are filled with Sai Baba's quotes in all possible languages. The energy was intense, and I particularly judged it as dense. However, I was the one feeling "dense" from all our traveling. My stomach was tight. The butterflies and the sensations were strong.

I had a lot of data about who Sai Baba was supposed to be. I knew him first from a discotheque in Acapulco. Over the main entrance, a picture of Sai Baba hung on the wall. I also had heard about him in the book, *The Bliss of Freedom*, where M. C. meets him, and Sai Baba sends him to Muktananda. Prema Baba relates experiences of Sai Baba in his book, *The Initiation*, as well. My beautiful friend Roberto, who lives in Cancun, has been Sai Baba's devotee for many years, having had the honor to participate in a couple of private sessions with him. Roberto calls Sai Baba, "The Father." I had heard many stories about Sai Baba randomly selecting someone from the crowd to have a private meeting with him. To be honest, I wanted to create that. Was it me that wanted that or was it my ego?

Finally, we arrived at the ashram: Prasanthi Nilayam in Anantapur Dt. The guards at the main gated entrance were beautifully dressed in white. It was almost 9 PM when we arrived, and the ashram was already closed. When I requested admittance, my dream came true. The answer was "NO!"

That was the first "no" that we had received, and the beginning of plenty of others we heard during our stay at [2]Prasanthi Nilayam. With an uncomfortable feeling in my mind, my stomach felt tense but, at the same time, I accepted what was happening and focused on learning the lesson being given. The driver took us to a small hotel very close to the ashram. Although small, it had three floors, and I thought: "Oh my God! There are probably no elevators here! Our bags are very heavy!"

I took a deep breath and prayed, "Please God, remind me of humbleness again." I stayed in the car while Govinda and Akshmil inspected the rooms to see if they would be appropriate for us. Bhakti called to me to look up at the window of one of the rooms. Three monkeys were there! Of course, I took that as a sign! The monkey is the symbol of one of the Hindu gods, [3]Hanuman. He was the

---

2.   Prasanthi Nilayam, the simple-looking two-story building of granite, was inaugurated on November 23, 1950, the twenty-fifth birthday of Baba. It has a central portion profusely strewn with sculptured flowers of all sizes In addition, there was a small portico attached to the central portion of the corridor in the front. Equally significant is the scene of the sculptured avatars adorning the walls of the hall, enacting the drama of divine descent and divine grace for the uplift of mankind. It is significant that all these avatars have upraised hands in the abhaya pose, conferring benediction on all those who are pure at heart. http://www.sathyasai.org/

King of the Monkey tribe who assisted Rama in saving Sita (his wife) from Ravana's kidnapping. I have a picture of Hanuman in my daughter's playroom in Mexico that was given to me as a gift during a visit to Alaska.

This was the place! When Govinda came back, he said that it was fine. Many people from the hotel assisted us with our bags. They were honored to have us stay with them and even offered us a discount for our rooms. Also, one of the owners had a travel agency and arranged a tour of Puttaparthi the next day. Our trip back to Bangalore on September 30 also was arranged.

Bhakti, Deva, and I shared a room, which was very clean and simple. The men shared another room. And, of course, our room happened to be the one where the monkeys peeked at us through the window. When we asked the manager about those three furry creatures, he said that they didn't belong to anyone. They were all around Puttaparthi, and no one knew when they would next appear.

That night as we mediated together, Ame gave us a message about the intense energy we were all feeling. Before judging it or complaining, she said, we should connect with our own Yang energy. We had been experiencing the Yin in the care of the Mother. Now it was time to make things happen, to use our Yang energy, and find a balance.

My friends and I were having "different" sensations. In Mexico, we call it *se te mueve el tapete* (the carpet is moving), which means only one thing: Take a good look at your stuff!

We went to sleep and woke up at 5:00 since we needed to be at the ashram at 6:30 AM sharp to prepare for *darshan*. Near dawn, we could hear the temple bell ringing first nine times, then five times, then once. It sounded like a church bell with loud and deep tones that reminded me of the churches in Mexico. The Vedic chanting began. We walked down the narrow street decorated with flowers and arrived to experience the ashram and the many rules it had.

We were walking all together in a group, and the guards stopped us to say: "You can't walk this way. You, women, go to the other side. You cannot take any bags into the ashram with you. You cannot sing out loud. You cannot take pictures here. You cannot, you cannot...you cannot!"

My friend Deva protested. In response, the guard began to give us his whole menu of nos. Deva had a burst of *Shakti* (energy) laughter that arose spontane-

---

3.    Hanuman is a monkey god. He is a noble hero and great devotee of Lord Rama of the Ramayana. This deity is a provider of courage, hope, knowledge, intellect, and devotion. He is pictured as a robust monkey holding a mace (gada), which is a sign of bravery, and having a picture of Lord Rama attached on his chest, which is a sign of his devotion to Lord Rama. http://hindunet.org/god/Gods/hanuman/

ously. It had nothing to do with the man who was only doing his job. Yet, I could tell that he did not like her laughter. His whole face frowned, and his white teeth remained hidden inside his mouth. Bhakti and I, like embarrassed mothers, walked away.

Finally, after all the security procedures, we arrived at the main temple to wait for Sai Baba and receive his *darshan*. Bhakti was not wearing a shawl. One of the female security guards, in a very intense tone, told her, "You cannot come in without a shawl on. It is very disrespectful!" Ahhhhh…, that's it! I began translating for Bhakti and found myself telling the security people lies!

I told them to please excuse my friend and to understand she had just arrived from Mexico and that her custom prohibited her wearing shawls. After I told this to three different women, they let us in. I didn't feel like lying, and I knew the consequences might manifest later but, in the meantime, we finally were inside the temple.

They directed us to a special place to be seated. In fact, they actually pulled us down to the floor. Where did they get so much strength in their arms? I began to experience the energy of the moment as I started to meditate and began to feel lighter in weight, not only physically, but also mentally. The energy inside it took another hour for Sai Baba to come out. When I opened my eyes, more than 50,000 people filled the area or meditation hall called the *Mandir* (living temple for the living god)

Then someone told us that we were very lucky that day (a phrase that all over our journey was constantly being repeated to us), for it had been two months since Sai Baba had given a public *darshan*.

Sai Baba was about to appear. All of us were very excited. There were people from all over the world, and the guards were eagle-eye attentive! They were not shy about pulling people down into a sitting position, because now and then a woman would dare to be brave enough to kneel! Sai Baba made his grand entrance, wearing his orange robe with his famous smile, seated in a type of golf cart. His driver took him all around the temple. He passed close by us. People were praying, pleading to him, and raising their hands to receive his blessings. Sai Baba just kept smiling, looking at everything and everyone around. Then he left! The darshan lasted ten minutes!

That day was the beginning of the nine-day Navaratri Festival, acknowledging the celebration of the Feminine Energy by honoring the Hindu goddesses. We walked out of the temple to have breakfast outside the ashram in a beautiful Italian restaurant. It was very clean with loving service, great tamarind sauce, and delicious rice bread! Then we went to take our tour of Puttaparthi. Unfortunately, because of the Navaratri celebration, everything was closed! Well…laughing a little, we decided to continue our tour and visit all the temples, although they were closed to visitors.

The only building that was open was a spiritual museum located on top of the hill on the southern side of the ashram. The main theme centered around the experience of spirituality in man's evolution. It displayed wonderful and fascinating objects that conveyed the eternal message of the masters, sages, and saints of all religions of the world. The stories of Bhagawan's (Sai Baba) early life and his declaration of being an Avatar were emphasized. On three floors, there were representations of the endless spiritual quest of man, regardless of race, time, and space; paintings that represented the different religions and world faiths. The architecture was a special style called [4]Shikara. We were like little children there, reading all the stories and looking at all the pictures. What surprised us most was a special area where Mexico was honored. A huge picture of the Mother of Guadalupe hung on the wall. Just as I said hello to her, they announced, "You must go, the museum is closed!"

We walked down the rocky hill, barefoot, to a huge banyan tree that was planted by Satya Sai Baba in 1950. We sat down for a while to meditate. A young boy approached me to buy some postcards. When he noticed I was silently meditating, he patiently waited. His energy was so respectful and he was so young that I decided to buy all of the postcards from him. He was a very clever young man, who at fifteen had taught himself English. He also was very good at explaining the story of the tree, so we invited him to be our guide for the day, and he did an amazing job. He took us for a long walk up the hill to the cave where Sai Baba used to meditate in his younger days. The view from above was fantastic. We could see the entire city from where we were: the temples, the people, and the deep blue sky. The place is considered very holy. We placed incense there and then took pictures on the top of the hill with our new young friend, Nibu.

Afterward, we went to visit the house where Satya Sai Baba was born. Then we had lunch in a wonderful Tibetan restaurant. Over the main entrance hung a picture of his Holiness the Dalai Lama. By then, every picture I saw of any guru, dead or alive, emanated a manifestation of blessings. Concepts like time, sect, and

---

4.    The Shikara style is characterized by a beehive-shaped tower (called a shikhara). It was developed in the 5th Century. It is made up of layer upon layer of architectural elements, such as kapotas and gavaksas, all topped by a large round cushion-like element called an amalaka. The plan is based on a square, but the walls are sometimes so broken up that the towers often give the impression of being circular. http://www.templenet.com/temparc.html

tradition were disappearing. For me, all was alive! Everything was a sacred magical message! I was drunk again with love and remained like that for many days.

The spicy food, rice, bread, curry vegetables, and lentils were fantastic, and the service, once again, was given with so much love that we gave thanks to the cook. Like Chinese Buddhas with big happy bellies, we went for a walk to buy some incense and then went back to our hotel.

After resting for a bit, we returned to the ashram for the 3 PM *darshan* with Sai Baba. This time, we were prepared. We went along with the rules and everything flowed more easily. Bhakti even brought her shawl! The afternoon *darshan* lasted an hour. I watched Sai Baba and mentally sent him thoughts of health and love. Then I said silently, "I would appreciate it if you would send me a sign that you are indeed listening to my commentaries. Please confirm that you've received my message." Sai Baba looked over to where I was sitting and nodded.

The play (*leela*) was beautiful! After *darshan*, we walked around the ashram only to discover what a huge city it was! It even had a shopping center. We tried to go in, but a guard stopped us by saying, "No women allowed!" Ha! That was perfect! It was now time for the men to do the shopping and a good lesson for the women to hold back, transcend, and evolve into the acceptance of the moment! We did, and we found the library to occupy our time.

The warmth red-yellow sunset was perfect. The birdsong was melodious, it sounded like a harp. We stayed in the garden, drank some soy milk, and quietly watched the sky until it got dark and the moon came out. We all went back to the hotel and had a meditation with Ame. A pizza arrived for our dinner that our beautiful friends from the hotel brought us!

The group at Puttaparthi with the young Nibu, the young child whose
wisdom was equal to an elder. © Mastery Life A.C

# Guru Brahma Story
## September 30

No matter what accomplishments you make, somebody helped you.
*~ Althea Gibson*

Deva was the only one who woke up early and went to *darshan* with Sai Baba. This was our last day, and our plane was leaving to Delhi from Bangalore at 4 PM At breakfast, Deva told us a funny story regarding her experience at *darshan* that day. She was obediently sitting quietly, as requested by the security people. When Sai Baba's golf cart passed in front of where she sat, she spontaneously stood up and started screaming, waving her arms, "Hey, Sai Baba!" The holy man, with grand amusement, smiled at her. Thirty seconds later she was entirely surrounded by security guards. They got her to sit down, saying many things to her in their own language. She naturally couldn't understand the words, so it was easy not to be identified with it or to take it personally. She was very blissful for the experience and for letting her heart free to create a memory that will last forever. Her "break the rules" nature is nearly always apparent.

Govinda, Akshmil, and I went to Sai Baba's house before we left. I had a mental conversation with him, explaining how my ego had really been catalyzed at his ashram with all the rules and control measures. Then I thanked him for receiving me there and that I was continuing my journey. I left a red rose in gratitude in front of the main entrance, and then we went back to the hotel.

As we arrived at the hotel, a voice inside my head said, "Leave your shoes right now as a gift to the man sitting outside!" Then, I thought, "Okay, I will, but not now." I was feeling lazy. And as soon as I tried to walk up the first step toward my room, one of my shoes slipped, and I fell down and hurt my knee very badly.

What was going on? Was I distracted? Was I disregarding the message I had just received? The manifestation was clear, so I turned around and made sure to give away both my shoes and my laziness.

While I was recuperating from my fall, I began to read some Indian stories. Here is one:

Once upon a time, in a beautiful forest, there was a hermitage in which the great Sage Dhaumya lived with all his disciples. One day, a boy came and bowed to the teacher and persuaded him to accept him as a disciple. That was a rare thing, because in those days the sage would decide which student to accept or not.

Dhaumaya noticed that the boy, Upamanyu, was dull and very slow. He was not interested in his studies and did not understand the scriptures. He also was not very obedient, but the Master loved him very much.

Upamanyu had a very hearty appetite. He loved to eat a lot. The sage noticed this tendency and addressed him so that *thamongana* (dullness) would not manifest in the boy's life.

To keep him focused, the Master told Upamanyu to take the ashram cows to graze early in the morning and return at sunset and to take a small lunch with him to the fields. However, the boy's appetite was huge. So when he milked the cows, he drank all the milk.

Dhaumaya noticed that Upamanyu was getting fatter each day. He questioned him and was told the truth about the milk. The Master explained to the boy that he was not allowed to do that without the guru's permission! Upamanyu agreed not to drink the milk, but his hunger was so strong that he noticed that the calves would drop milk whenever they suckled their mothers. So the boy collected the drops and drank it. After a while, the teacher noticed that Upamanyu was not getting any thinner and questioned the boy once again. Upamanyu again told him the truth.

The Master explained that what he did was not a clean thing. The milk was contaminated and could harm his health. So Upamanyu once more promised not to do it. Yet, he couldn't control his hunger. One afternoon he saw some fruits in a tree. He ate them all. These fruits, however, were poisonous, and he immediately became blind! Upamanyu panicked and began to run but, since he couldn't see, he fell into a deep well.

The cows went back to the hermitage by themselves at milking time, and Master Dhaumaya went to look for his disciple. After much searching, he found him and got him out of the well. The sage felt so much compassion for Upamanyu that he gave him a mantra that eventually healed his sight.

Upamanyu received a great lesson from the Master: "Greediness always leads to disaster." This time the disciple learned his lesson and felt more love for his Master than ever.

In this story, Master Dhaumya behaves as the Hindu trinity. He is *BRAHMA* when he created love from the disciple to the Master. He is *VISHNU* (The Protector) when he saved him from the well. And he acted as *SHIVA* (Maheshwara) when he destroyed the bad qualities of greed, guiding his disciple toward liberation.

The *bhajan* or *stotra* chanted from this story praises all the names of the Divine:

*GURU BRAHMA, GURU VISHNU,*
*GURU DEVO, MAHESHVARAH,*
*GURU SAKSHAT, PARA BRAHMA,*
*TASMAI SHREE GURAVE NAMAH.*

Swami Govinda and Bhaktiananda meditating at the top of the hill in
Puttaparthi where it is said that Satya Sai Baba attained Enlightenment.
© Mastery Life A.C

# To Bangalore

Cheerfulness and contentment are great beautifiers and
are famous preservers of youthful looks.
~ *Charles Dickens*

On our way back to Bangalore, our driver made a stop. (One of many that are
usually not announced to the people inside the car!) He stopped at a very small
temple where a *sannyasin* came and blessed us with *tilak* and gave us *prasad*, while
the driver was blessing his car with coconut water for a safe trip. Later, we
stopped at what I consider one of the most beautiful temples I've ever seen. Very
similar to Chichen Itza in Mexico, the temple was very ancient and where some
of the episodes of the [5]Ramayana occurred, or so the stories said. The story could
be seen carved in stone. We heard amazing stories (by a spontaneous guide that
manifested at our side) regarding the architects of the place and how they built a
grand cobra statue in no more than a week! The size of that cobra was approximately twelve feet tall. The carved stones, the footsteps of Garuda, the bird that
released Sita (Rama's wife), the Wedding Hall, the Dancing Hall—these places
were absolutely blinding in their energy and beauty.

We saw an unfinished temple there. The main architect had died inside, and
the blood from his eyes is still painted on the rocks. Ahhhhh...just imagining the
moment took my breath away! After our tour, we arrived back inside the main
temple just in time for puja, prasad, and coconut milk. Ahhhhh, delicious! A
*pujari* also gave me two bananas and said, "Give these to the monkey." I agreed,
although we were in a little rush to get back to Bangalore for our flight. We hur-
ried outside, and a monkey ran fast, heading directly toward me. A "data" sur-
faced in my mind regarding a story Govinda told me of how he was badly beaten
by a monkey once. The mind is so quick! So much focus and attentiveness is
needed at every moment! When the running monkey approached me, one of my
friends screamed so loud, I jumped. I threw the bananas on the ground. The
monkey grabbed them and ran away. My heartbeat was the fastest ever, and the

---

5.    One of the two great epics of Indian literature, telling the story of one of Vishnu's
      avatars known as Rama. The Ramayana tells the story of Rama and his wife Sita (the
      ideal domestic couple), Sita's abduction by the demon Ravana, and her rescue with
      the help of the monkey king Hanuman (who is later made into a god) and his mon-
      key army. www.aar-site.org/syllabus/syllabi/c/cannon/r201glos.htm

laughter of the moment was even better! That is why all spiritual teachers say: Always be attentive and watch.

Devananda, Swami Amenanda, and Akshmilandaji standing in front of
the sacred Cobra of the Seven Heads, which was said to be built in only
one week by two brothers and was created from single piece of stone.
© Mastery Life A.C

# New Delhi
## September 30 to October 5

*Internal peace is an essential first step to achieving peace in the world.*
*How do you cultivate it? It's very simple.*
*In the first place by realizing clearly that all mankind is one, that human beings in*
*every country are members of one and the same family.*
*~ His Holiness the Dalai Lama*

We arrived in New Delhi at The Oberoi Hotel, a very refined place and perhaps the best hotel in India. Our representative was with us arranging everything! The treatment was again divine. Whenever we tried to ask if we needed to do anything, the response would be, "Don't worry, everything is okay, Ma'am."

All during our journey, my two traveling numbers kept manifesting—numbers nine and eleven. They were either my room number, my seat on the airplane, a bill to pay—whatever. Of course, my room number was 128 which, if you add it, is eleven. Once a friend of mine told me that the number eleven represented the Master, the guru, and that number nine was perfection. In the Hindu tradition, the number nine is highly respected.

This time I had a room to myself. Having roommates during the whole trip had been nice. It was a very good lesson for me—sharing, teamwork, and respecting the space of others. Nevertheless, I was very happy to have my own space this time.

I first created my altar and lit some incense. I gave thanks to be there and then went to explore the town. That night, Alex and I went to a restaurant at the top of the hotel and had an amazing Chinese dinner. We had a humble conversation together, reflecting in each other the things we needed to be more focused on and the aspects we needed to work. Alex is one of my best and dearest friends and, like brother and sister, the bond has grown deeper and deeper, always pointing each other toward the miracle and magic of existence.

That night I dreamt that I was walking in a green field that was covered with white rose petals. The sky was filled with lotus flowered clouds and a beautiful Indian woman was looking at me. She took my hand and walked me in to a palace that suddenly appeared: It was the Taj Mahal.

# Divine Love Story
## Agra, the Capital of the Mughal Monarchs
## October 1

Singing a song, the spirit dances.
Loving your creation, I am here, now.
~ *Ivonne Delaflor* ·

At 7 AM sharp, we headed to Agra with our "strong in character and focused mind" driver, Mr. Rana. There were many cows all over the place! In Mexico, we have dogs eating the trash from the streets, begging for food, and so on. Here, they have cows. I knew that cows were considered sacred in India. They are related to Krishna and the *gopis*, Krishna's cowherd devotees. However, I noticed that sometimes people would push them away. I felt compassion for the cows because they were absolutely beautiful and, if I may say, extremely self-sufficient. They (and the pigs) ate whatever was in the street.

The traffic was light since we were driving early in the morning, and the route was wonderful. I delighted in watching the small temples that passed by, and I was amazed that most of the temples were grave markers from different Sheiks or Maharishis that used to rule there. Agra is like the New York of India but, instead of high buildings, it has temples. In New York, you see a lot of pigeons. Here, you see cows.

Agra has stoplights and traffic rules, unlike other cities in south India where things such as stoplights are purely decorative items on the roads. Signs say: "We like you, but not your speed. Respect the Traffic Rules." What type of rules were those? Maybe, the true meaning of those rules was: Save your life, make sure the brakes work in your car! And maybe also, don't forget to sound the horn whenever a car is five centimeters away from crashing into yours! Wow. Driving in India could be really hazardous to your health unless you carry the power of Trust. I see it as lifetime insurance!

The long trees and the orange rising sun that looked like a sunflower to me was this miracle seen and remembered by all people in the world. I observed everyone working: the men carrying fruit to sell, the women cooking, the children gathering firewood. The rickshaw drivers were dusting off their carts. I saw human beings in India, doing the best that they could, just like everywhere in the world.

Our drive was mostly silent. Sometimes we were chanting, and sometimes Alex would delight us with his endless jokes that burst our hearts and minds into laughter. He told wonderfully refined jokes with such grace like this one:

*It is pouring rain in the flood plain of the Mississippi Valley, and the rising river begins to threaten all manner of private homes, including that of the local Rabbi.*
*With water coming into the ground floor, a rowboat with police comes by, and the officer shouts, "Rabbi, let us evacuate you! The water level is getting dangerous."*
*The Rabbi replies, "No thank you. I am a righteous man, who trusts in the Almighty, and I am confident he will deliver me." Three hours go by, and the rains intensify, at which point the Rabbi has been forced up to the second floor of his house. A second police rowboat comes by, and the officer shouts, "Rabbi, let us evacuate you! The water level is getting dangerous."*
*The Rabbi replies, "No thank you. I am a righteous man, who trusts in the Almighty, and I am confident he will deliver me."*
*The rain does not stop, and the Rabbi is forced up onto the roof of his house. A helicopter flies over, and the officer shouts down, "Rabbi, grab the rope, and we'll pull you up! You're in terrible danger!"*
*The Rabbi replies, "No thank you. I am a righteous man, who trusts in the Almighty, and I am confident he will deliver me."*
*The deluge continues, and the Rabbi is swept off the roof, carried away in the current and drowns. He goes up to heaven, and at the Pearly Gates he is admitted, and comes before the Divine Presence.*
*The Rabbi asks, "Dear Lord, I don't understand. I've been a righteous observant person my whole life and depended on you to save me in my hour of need. Where were you?"*
*And the Lord answered, "I sent two boats and a helicopter, what more do you want?"*

All our moments were spiritual, and the jokes were a meditation of laughter itself! I tried to tell my jokes, but the laughter of my friends came because of my inexperience in telling them.

Our driver enlightened us with his knowledge of the roads and the temples we passed. [6]There was a long line of picturesque ghats, with their steps leading to the water's edge, arched gateways, and temple spires extending along the right bank of the River Yamuna.

---

6.    http://www.pilgrimage-india.com/north-india-pilgrimage/mathura.html

I went into a meditative state, and I had a vision of Krishna's beautiful blue figure. His blue complexion reminded me of the Cancun Ocean, his black locks of hair shined like stars, lotus flower garlands were around his neck, and a seductive smile on his face. At that moment, the driver announced we were in Mathura, Krishna's birthplace. My heart was palpitating strongly. A loud voice inside me—my higher self or inner voice—told me to take a piece of paper and write a message:

The voice said, "In time, we will give you the information for a document that you shall create. The title is and has always been *Babaji Speaks to the Parents of the World.* Then a TABLE OF CONTENTS was "given" to me:

CHAPTER I: THE PARENT AS A SACRED TOOL
The Mission Revealed
The Frequency of Intention
Mastering the Mind through Love

CHAPTER II: DIVINE CHILD
Breathing and Breathing
Welcome to Earth
Possible Choices
The Meditative Toy
Selecting a [7]*Siddhi*

CHAPTER III: TEACHERS
Be Quiet
Blessing the Feet of the Disciple
The Voice of the Heart
The Thunderbolt—Guidance
Letting Go

CHAPTER IV: GOD'S REALIZATION
I Am

---

7.    Siddhi is an ability that is activated in the super-conscious field of the mind. These different abilities include the expression of the soul's genius in human life, such as the gift of inspired musical ability or mastery of a scientific discipline. It may confer a heightening of inner sensing, expand intuitive knowledge, activate miraculous powers, and grant the ability to minister the Light to others.
www.mudrashram.com/glossarypage.html

You Are
Welcome to Reality
No-Time Experience
Always by Your Side
Humbleness

CHAPTER V: IMMORTALITY
Just Believe
Eating Love
The Twelve Gates of Knowledge
I'll Be Waiting for You
The New Light Beings
The Whirling Gate of the Eternal Cycles

I was in tears receiving this special gift of information. Questions began to arise: Why me? And then: Why not? I did not want my ego to praise herself for this! But could it be real? Was this truly happening? I took a deep breath, listening to the inner voice saying, "I will guide you."

I took another deep breath and looked forward to arriving in Agra. We made a stop to pick up our guide, Mr. Joshi. During our time together, his gratitude to be with us was always apparent. Time and time again, every guide and every driver would create a special bond with us, and each of them offered a special teaching, a special message.

I was eager to arrive at the Taj Mahal. I had been longing to visit it since I was twelve years old. Finally my dream of visiting it was becoming a reality, and the reality was grander than the dream.

# The Taj Mahal
## Monument of Eternal Love

All my life I've been looking for you,
early childhood, womb…forever.
~ *Ivonne Delaflor*

The Taj Mahal is not only considered one of the marvels of the world, but also was built as a reminder to a great love story. When we stepped out of the car, we were immediately approached by photographers bargaining for their services, and we decided to take the official tourist picture inside the grandiose monument.

The Taj is a mausoleum built by an order of the Mughal Emperor, Shah Jajan. He requested its construction as an offering to the memory of his most beloved wife, Arjumand Banu Bagam. (The emperor later gave her the name, Mumtaz, The Exalted One.)

With her death in 1632, the sorrow of the emperor was so grand; he vowed to make a monument to the beauty of his wife. Hers was not only an external beauty but an internal beauty as well. He wanted everyone to always remember her. She was his wife, his friend, his counselor, and always inspired him with her loving heart in acts of charity toward those in need. He commanded the beginning of the construction.

Our guide, Mr. Joshi, explained that the meaning of the word *Taj* is not clear. It translates as either "Crown Palace" or "Crown of the Palace," but it is also, if you are attentive to the name, an abbreviated version of her name, Mumtaz Mahal, the Exalted One of the Palace. It took twenty-two years to build.

I couldn't stop thinking of this love. Could a love be so grand between a man and a woman that a symbol of that love could persevere, despite all odds, through eons of time? I don't know how long the Taj Mahal will delight us with its presence but, most definitely, the love that once was could be felt even now. I felt something so familiar. Somehow, I knew the place. It was not a strange "new" view, but something I already knew. I gazed at the wonderful scene of the southern bank of the [8]Yamuna River.

The Taj is built completely in white marble, and its composition is made of four identical facades, each containing a large central arch. A huge bulb-shaped dome rises over the center. It is flanked by two red sandstone buildings: a mosque and its replica, the *Jawab* (Answer). The main function of the *Jawab* is for visual balance. The whole mausoleum is a treasure of wisdom and beauty, decorated with inscriptions from the Muslim holy book, the *Koran* (Qur'an). Everything is symmetrically perfect. The perfect green gardens are heaven themselves, mathematically exact and in harmony with the whole construction. Our guide explained that the design of the garden is a Muslim symbol of paradise centered on a large, raised pool.

Canals divide the mausoleum into four equal parts, each containing flower-beds, fountains, and cypress trees, which are symbols of death.

Inside is the tomb of Mumtaz Mahal at the center of an octagonal hall. A slightly larger tomb of Shah Jahan (who died in 1666) is off to one side. Both are elaborately carved and inlaid with semiprecious stones and illuminated by sunlight filtering through a delicately carved marble screen also studded with jewels.

Many consider the story of Mumtaz a sad one. For me, it's a true celebration not only of eternal love, but also of life and death itself. Everything about the place continued to be very familiar to me.

Inside the mausoleum, through the crowd, I saw a man, dressed in orange, with black hair and perfect white teeth. He smiled and kept looking at me. The energy was intense. I looked back at him and waved and offered him a silent *Namaste*. As we continued our walk, I saw him again. I was about to ask him, "Do I know you?" But, at that same moment, he waved at me in *Namaste* and looked directly into my eyes, smiled, and nodded. I turned my head to see where my friend Alex was, and when I looked back for the man, he was gone.

The time came to leave, but not before we sat in the gardens and had an appropriate meditation. Ame shared her message with all, and then it was time for a nutritious and meditative lunch. Mr. Joshi took us to a local restaurant, where the owner treated us like family. The way we were attended to added flavor to our already delicious food. In India, hospitality is sacred. You can learn more about it in their sacred texts or in *The Tirukural*, an ethical masterpiece composed in [9]*Tamil* by the Saint Tiruvalluvar. It is a compendium of practical advice, the Bible on Virtue for the Human Race. Here is one little taste from Chapter IX:

---

8.    Originating from the Champasar Glacier at an altitude of 4421 m in the state of Uttarkhand, the revered Yamuna finds a special mention in the Hindu mythology. Some say the source of the river is the Saptarishi Kund, a glacial lake. There is a sacred shrine of Yamunotri or Yamnotri near this source at an altitude of 3235 m. There is a temple dedicated to the Goddess Yamuna, which remains closed from November to May. At Hanumanchatti, the Hanuman Ganga merges with Yamuna River. According to a legend, this secluded hilly spot was the home of an ancient sage, Asit Muni.
       http://www.pilgrimage-india.com/holy-rivers/jamuna-yamuna-river.html

*The whole purpose of earning wealth and maintaining a home*
*is to provide hospitality to guests.*
*If a man cares daily for those who come to him,*
*his life will never suffer the grievous ruin of poverty.*

Outside a young boy and his father danced. They were dressed in beautiful red clothes and moved their eyes and heads as if they were made out of rubber! After lunch, we began to shop. In a small store, the artisans showed us the wonderful process of marble inlaid of semiprecious stones on plates, boxes, ashtrays, and furniture. They use seashells and stones for the inlay process: jasper, mother-of-pearl, turquoise, lapis lazuli, and carnelian. They glue them in a special, secret process from natural cement created with plants and stones—a secret kept for centuries!

Alex was approached by one of the salespeople who was very attracted to his energy. Alex's generosity manifested, and he did an astrology reading for him. The man was so grateful. His deep olive green eyes were shining love. Alex's spoken words to this man were filled with love and humbleness.

We stopped at another store owned by a friend of Mr. Joshi's. My friends found some beautiful things, and I found that the owner was a very spiritual being. As I was looking at some jewels and chanting some mantras, he came to me and said, "I don't know who you all are, but my heart rejoices with your presence. You and your friends give me great peace." Then Mr. Joshi told us that his friend was considered very wise, learned of the scriptures, and very psychic. He requested our blessings for his business, and he wished blessings for us.

While we were saying farewell, Mr. Joshi approached me and gave me a beautiful white marble elephant with jewels inlaid on it. At first, I thought he wanted to sell it but, before I opened my mouth, he said, "It is a gift for you. You and your friends have blessed me. You are my first tourists since September 11, 2001." He asked, "Could you bless me? I would like to be part of your work and your organization! Please!" I prayed silently with tears in my eyes and focused on humbleness.

This man had such a humble way! My legs weakened, and I asked him how he knew about our work? He replied, "I can feel, too." We exchanged e-mail

---

9.   * Tamil's origins are independent of Sanskrit (which is from the Indo-European language family and the ancestor of many Indian languages). Tamil is one of the Dravidian languages. It is one of the Classical languages of the world. http://en.wikipedia.org/wiki/Tamil_language

addresses and said farewell to Mr. Joshi, Agra, and we forever welcomed the energy of eternal love.

The group at the Taj Mahal. © Mastery Life A.C

# Mathura

HARE KRISHNA, HARE KRISHNA,
KRISHNA KRISHNA, HARE HARE,
HARE RAMA, HARE RAMA
RAMA RAMA, HARE HARE

The devotees of Lord Krishna try to chant this mantra every moment of every day. It is suggested to chant it at least sixteen rounds a day. It is known as the great mantra for it contains the Holy Name of God as Krishna.

On our way to Mathura, my heart was beating so strongly. We drove for two hours, and we could barely see the landscape. When we arrived, it was already very dark. The small town was full of people celebrating *Navaratri*. In the main temple, where it is said that Krishna was born, a puja was being held in honor of the Goddess [10]Durga.

Our driver, Mr. Rana, parked, and in this crowded city we had to walk to the temple. We were uncertain as to how to get there and what to do. Mr. Rana couldn't accompany us because he needed to wait with the car. A stranger approached us, offering to serve as our guide. For the first time, a doubt and a discomfort arose in me. Nevertheless, everyone else decided that it was okay for him to assist us.

The temple was full and the entrance was packed with people. Our guide said, "Follow me." A shiver came into my body. Was it good or bad? We walked to the back of the temple. It looked like an alley; a narrow street that seemed to have no way out. My mind began to create fear. No people were around, and I was feeling more than a little uncomfortable. Thoughts regarding insecurity, thieves, and fear arose. The way to enter the temple was already behind us.

The sensation reminded me of when my husband and I went to Bangkok, one of the most crowded cities in the world. One day we had an appointment in thirty minutes, and we were far from where we needed to be. With traffic, it would take no less than two hours to get there. A man approached us and said, "I

---

10.    The goddess Durga, whose name means etymologically, "One who can redeem in situations of utmost distress," performs her saving deeds in infinite and often times imperceptible ways. She is known first and foremost as a slayer of demons. When the malevolent Buffalo Demon, Mahisa, had forcefully taken the heavens and earth away from the gods, it was she whom Brahma, Vishnu, and Siva created to defeat him and restore order in the universe.
http://www.courses.rochester.edu/muller-ortega/rel249/durga/yoga.html

will make sure you both get there on time. Your wife can go on one motorcycle, and you can use another!" We wanted to go together, but the man insisted on separating us.

For my husband, being on time for the appointment, which was actually a doctor's appointment for me, was very important. He decided to take the man's offer to get there faster and, of course, I followed on another motorcycle. Everything was fine. We rode accompanying each other. Two motorcycles, two drivers who did not speak English, and two Mexicans were in a rush to get to a destination as fast as possible. The guy driving my motorcycle turned left into what seemed to be an alley. Oh my God, I thought. My mind was caught in a thriller movie. I believed I was going to be kidnapped and sold. Maybe raped or killed! I couldn't ask the driver why he had turned, and I couldn't ask him where my husband was! He drove through the streets full of pedestrians running away from the motorcycle. My fear was so intense that I said, "Okay, if this is my last moment on Earth, I'd better enjoy it."

Freedom manifested for me. I began enjoying the people screaming at each other, the pollution of the cars and buses, the crowd, even the fast driving of my driver! In no more than ten minutes, I arrived at my destination! I couldn't believe it. My husband's driver took a bit longer. He had first returned to the place where he last saw me.

But you should have seen the look on my husband's face when he finally arrived. He hugged me strongly, and relief gave color to his skin once again!

Now, we arrived at a special entrance, which was a shortcut to the main temple. See? Not everything is what it seems. Trust, before you get lost in your own mind! Relief not only covered my face but on my companions' faces as well.

We arrived exactly on time for the last part of the puja. Once again, we were able to chant and participate in it. It was beautiful. We walked to what is said to be the jail in which Lord Krishna was born. Yasodara, Krishna's mother, and her husband were jailed by her brother, Kansa, the fearful king who knew Yasodara's child would be, according to the prophecies, the grandest king of all time. Kansa was jealous, and he put his sister in jail so that when her baby was born, he could kill him. But Yasodara secretly put the baby in a basket and gave it to two humble beings who raised Krishna with grand love in their simple environment. Krishna was known for his great spiritual manifestations and also for stealing butter and milk to give to the poor. As a young man, he was also very great king.

I have always felt a special connection with Krishna. I've always admired his beauty, the wisdom expressed in the *Bhagavad-Gita*, his romance with Radha, his Shakti, and the music of his flute. I have loved the cows and peacocks that surround the paintings of him. Krishna is said to be the Divine incarnation of Lord Vishnu.

Inside the jail, which is the main attraction of Mathura, is the *Shri Krishna Janmbhoomi* (Lord Krishna's birthplace). A quarry stone marks the exact spot where Krishna was born.

The energy created from my beliefs, the devotees praying, and the celebration of being there delivered a great meditation for all of us. Before our trip to India, we received a message that said we needed to go to Mathura. No reasons were given; we were just requested to go.

It was getting really late, but we decided to go to the city of Brindavan (also called Vrindaban), which is only twenty km away from Mathura. It is said that Lord Krishna lived his childhood there. The place is very beautiful, large pine trees adorned the road along with temples and people dressed in white—the energy was peaceful. Brindavan is said to have many, many temples! We arrived at the main temple of ISKON, the Hare Krishna Movement's ashram.

It was all marble and perfectly clean. There were guest rooms for people who wished to stay. We saw many young people from all over the world. We arrived exactly when they were doing the last part of the puja, the *arati*. Again, we participated while the music was chanted by the devotees and community members sang Hare Krishna!

When the puja ended, the temple closed. We met a new friend from Venezuela, who was smiling from one ear to the other, expressing his love and service for the Divine teachings of Shri Krishna.

The temple was founded by A.C. Bhaktivedanta Swami Prabhupada. A temple was built in his honor, and a wax figure of him stood inside. I was interested in his face and name. I thought I had heard about him before. I was feeling intoxicated. The music, the puja—everything was perfect wine from the Divine.

Upon my return to the Western world, I decided to study the *Bhagavad-Gita*. I happened to have a very beautiful book, well-translated and well-written, that my dearest friend Sergio gave me as a gift. He told me that he was in a gas station fueling his car, and a young man came to sell his used books. My friend bought this book and stored it in his house. Years later we became very good friends, and one day he arrived with a gift that he felt was perfect for me. Of course, it was the *Bhagavad-Gita*. Not surprisingly, the author of this version I had in my hands was A.C Bhaktivedanta Swami Prabhupada. So, is that how we had met before?

Blissful and Krishna-ful, we headed back to Delhi, praising the amazing driving skills of Mr. Rana—always attentive, always respectful, and very protective of us. At 10:30 PM we arrived in Delhi and into Morpheo's arms once again.

# Sri Aurobindo's Ashram
## Delhi Branch

In a moment my mind became silent as a windless air
on a high mountain summit
and then I saw one thought and then another coming in
a concrete way from outside;
I flung them away before they could enter and
take hold of the brain and in three days I was free.
~ *Sri Aurobindo*

This ashram has been created with another object than that is ordinarily common
to such institutions, not for the renunciation of the world, but as a centre and
field of practice for the evolution of another kind and form of life which would in
the final end be moved by a higher spiritual consciousness and embody
a greater life of the spirit.
~ *Sri Aurobindo*

On October 2 it seemed that we already had been in India for a long time. We
went to visit Old Delhi first for an appointment at Sri Aurobindo's ashram. Since
we had arrived late, our appointment had been cancelled, but nevertheless we
decided to stay to meditate at the ashram and then continue our journey. I was
really pleased with the information that we received while in the library there. My
attention was directed to the many books they had for parents. I saw a picture of
Sri Aurobindo and his energy emanated certainty, elegance, and knowledge as
reflected in his teachings.

Sri Aurobindo, born in 1872, had his *Mahasamadhi* (conscious death) in
1950. He has been recognized as one of the most important revolutionary leaders
of India. He was a humanist, a visionary, a poet, and a *Rishi* (a Master of Yoga).
Sri Aurobindo completed his professional studies in England. Later he became
part of the revolutionary movement in India in 1906 and wrote a journal, *Bande
Mataram*, which became the strongest voice of the freedom movement. In 1910,
he renounced politics to pursue his spiritual life. With all his studies and experiences, he united spirit and matter in his teachings.

He wrote many books that promoted a visionary view of the world to come
and the evolutionary process. Aurobindo's insights were accurate and full of love.
In 1926, he began his total renunciation and left *Mira Alfassa* (later known as

The Mother) as the main mentor and guiding light for all Sri Aurobindo's disciples.

The books and the relaxed yet disciplined mood of the ashram awakened in me the sensation that I was being guided and prepared. But for what? I did not know.

Sri Aurobindo's ashram makes no distinctions of sex, creed, race, or religion. All people are souls and are children of the Divine Mother. There is no hierarchy. They have a meditation hall, regular lectures and workshops, a library, celebrations during the year, and a homeopathic dispensary with free medical care.

At the bookstore, we met with the last closest disciple of The Mother. About eighty-seven years old, his smile and peaceful energy were very refreshing. Before leaving, we went to the meditation hall where I had a very deep experience. My meditation took me to a place where there was no floor, no ceiling—just space. I did not hear any noise; there was no other being around me. The warmth began to manifest again. Sitting in front of a picture of Sri Aurobindo, I experienced that nothing ever dies! Perhaps the body has an expiration date, but the soul never dies. I felt Sri Aurobindo as alive as I was. In an empty space, all space exists, right?

When I opened my eyes, I walked directly toward a small shrine in the center of the garden. I knelt without any mental command and went into a deep state. I smelled an intoxicating fragrance, a combined elixir of rose, jasmine, and sandalwood, and tasted something sweet on my tongue.

For Bhakti and Govinda the ashram created more ideas for the Conscious Community they are developing called AME, (Awareness=Meditation=Energy) on a beautiful piece of land they own in the magical Mayan jungle. Seven cenotes, sacred caves full of crystalline blue water, are there.

For Alex, the message from The Mother created an opening regarding feminine energy. For me, I now had contact information and an e-mail address for Auroville, an amazing conscious, ecological community.

As soon as I got back from India, I contacted the main architect to request guidance for the development of the AME Community Center. The response was immediate. They were not only willing to assist and stay open to any possibility, but also the architect, Satprem, maintained (in his energy) a sacred reencounter of friendship and love. Satprem (Truth and Love) and I have developed a beautiful "electronic" friendship. He has been one of the most direct beings I've ever met. Honest, respectful, and an amazing poet, he is definitely a trustworthy friend.

The day Satprem, who is a devotee of Shiva, contacted me, I received a beautiful ring in the mail. It is called *rasamani,* and it is made of solidified mercury. The friends who sent this rare and beautiful gift wanted to express their thanks for some gifts I had brought them from India, but far beyond that was the gratitude I felt for our blessed friendship. They told me that if the ring was too small or too big I could hang it around my neck, for it had great healing properties. It is believed that the mercury can assist the one who wears it in whatever endeavor or situation one encounters. It is said that *rasamani* is the semen of Lord Shiva. The ring fit me perfectly. I kissed it and put it on my finger.

# Mr. J. Joseph

*With my wings open and my heart receiving*
*I am willing to accept all that I am.*
*~ Malena Alvarez*

We arrived that evening at the hotel, and the wonderful Mr. J. Joseph was waiting for us along with Suma, his beautiful wife. As soon as I walked into the lobby, he offered me a bouquet of flowers. His eyes were shining like a child's. He was as exited as we were to finally meet. Mr. Joseph is a very honoring and talented man.

We invited him and his wife to dinner. We praised him, expressing our gratitude for the amazing contacts he made for us. Then we shared our stories and gave him some gifts from Mexico. His respectful attitude and loving eyes were a treasure to behold. What our hearts had felt about him, our eyes were able to see and validate. I felt honored by his presence. Out of curiosity, I asked about his religion. He told me he was a Catholic and believed in the love and teachings of Jesus to guide his life.

Before coming to India, many people gave me images of deities or teachers to take with me. Two months before I left, I was at my doctor's office. Chris Kauffman is not only a great doctor and healer, but he also is a very honest and straightforward being and my friend. He and his wife, the beautiful and spiritual Melissa, live their lives guided by the Divine teachings of Jesus. When I first met him, I was attracted to a painting he had of Jesus. It was beautiful and captured the radiance of Jesus himself. I was so drawn toward it that Chris noticed and, in his generosity, couldn't help but give it to me as a gift in that moment. It was such an honor! Now the picture is in my children's sleeping room.

The day before leaving for India, I met a woman in Chris's office. A beautiful lady, her eyes had a special light. Chris introduced me to her as the painter of "the Jesus." I expressed my delighted feelings to her and explained about the experience I had of a light coming from the painting embracing me. She took from her bag a postcard with the image of the painting and gave it to me as a gift. I carried the postcard with me to India, and now Jesus was manifesting once again.

Mr. Joseph was teaching us about respect, honor, and devotion and demonstrating to us, without spoken words, the Divine message of love that was Jesus's teaching. I felt the presence not only of Jesus, but also the gratitude of meeting with such beautiful beings as Mr. Joseph and Suma. The message of love is always manifesting for us. Following my heart was again not only divinely perfect, but also humbling. Here was the validation that trust is a blessed tool.

# A Lesson of Trust
## October 3

*Worrying about something that may never happen*
*is like paying interest on money you may never borrow.*
*~ Unknown*

I woke feeling a little distressed. My visa, which is separate from my passport, had a different number than my passport. Suddenly, I panicked, imagining that somehow I could have problems going back into the U.S. before continuing to Mexico. Then I couldn't see my children again. Immediately I followed my "panic's advice" and called Alex. We headed to the Mexican Embassy because I was certain that I needed another visa.

I had to do everything in a very short period of time, which was very stressful. We needed to go to the bank. That was a lesson of wait and practice patience. Then Alex and I went to the embassy. They told me after an hour to come back tomorrow with this paper and that signature and so on.

Ahhhhh. We were leaving in just two days! No chance existed for me to even get my visa in that short time. Did that mean I needed to stay in India longer? That meant staying by myself. That meant more and more data and panic in my head. However, I was playing it cool. I mean, here I was in front of my friend! Ha! The fear of not seeing and kissing my children again in two days was strong. When I was with the woman at the embassy, suddenly I realized, "Wait a minute! I've been traveling like this for five years now! Of course! Computers have the records of everything—even my last passport and its number." I let go of my fear. To be honest, though, each time I handed my visa to any officer on our way home, the fear arose again for me. Yet, I had absolutely no problem at all.

After that illusory experience, Alex and I went to the Maharishi Ayurvedic Center. Alex and I had both being feeling a call to go to Rishikesh, five hours north of Delhi. We did not exactly know why, but both of us felt a strong pull to go. However, we were almost ready to leave India—two more days—so how could a trip there be arranged? We told ourselves that perhaps on our next visit to India we would include a visit to Rishikesh.

Our driver, an elegant man dressed in white, named Habir, was a beautiful, wise, and spiritual being. He enlightened us with his experiences, of marriage, spiritual thirst, and his feelings of love for the Divine.

Habir then asked Alex about God and the Soul. He shared with us how his spiritual focus was sometimes a problem with his wife who thought his yearning for God was nonsense. Then something happened, I don't know how, but suddenly our driver said, "You should go to Rishikesh. I was born there."

Alex and I just looked at each other and mentally agreed to go. Then the driver continued, "You know, a Master once stayed in my humble house. He is very old…I think 300 years or more." (By this time, Alex's eyes and mine were huge wide-open windows—like owl's eyes.) "He came to my house, slept with us, and he lives on only air. He can be seen in many places." Then he said, "I'll show you a picture of him that I have from a book created with his wisdom. Do you want to see it?"

We screamed, "YES!"

The picture of the holy man was very beautiful. He had long hair, sparkling eyes, and was dressed in white. Both Alex and I thought we were called by Babaji.

I still had questions such as: Is this possible? I am no guru. Is this real? Can an ordinary person meet with Babaji? Ahhhhh. Anyway, I decided to go to Rishikesh. We called our beloved Mr. Joseph who had actually recommended the previous night that we go to Rishikesh. Mr. Joseph had said, "It is only five hours away, and it is so close to the Himalayas." (My heart felt shivers.) When I called him to say we would like to go, we agreed upon returning the same day. He told us we had to leave very early to make the most of our time. All my friends agreed with my new crazy adventure, which led us to be the guests of magic and eternal life itself.

After all the arrangements were made for the following day, it was time to leave to go to the Shanti Mandir at Greenfield's School, where we would have the honor to meet with Swami Nityananda.

# Swami Nityananda
## The Joyful Soul
## Mahamandaleshwar

*When we meditate or chant we are not trying to bring truth to our level;
rather, we are elevating ourselves to the experience of what truth is.*
*~ Swami Nityananda*

We arrived at the Greenfield's School at 4:00. Mr. Ashok, a devotee and assistant of Swami Nityananda, invited us to participate in the ceremony that was going to take place. Inside the school were pictures of Swami Nityananda and Swami Muktananda, his beloved teacher and well-known guru. Swami Muktananda Paramahansa used to teach, *"Meditate on yourself. God dwells within you. See God in each other."* Nityananda's teachings are based on the teachings of Muktananda through chanting, meditation workshops, and endless selfless service all around the world.

I knew of Swami Nityananda because of my first teacher, a disciple and a good friend of Muktananda himself. How I got to meet him in India, however, had to do with the invitation of Mrs. Delia Amezquita. She lives in Mexico and is a disciple of Swami Nityananda. We've met only through the magic of the Internet. She has been nothing but positive, loving, and from her written words her deep spiritually can be felt.

When she knew I was coming to India, she immediately told me that I should meet with Swami Nityananda. She explained that it was a beautiful opportunity and that I would have the blessing to participate at the Navaratri Festival. She then quickly contacted all of her friends and had amazing patience with me, adjusting to my constant changes in schedule while in India and e-mailing her friends to announce my arrival. I am very grateful to her. What I experienced with Nityananda was absolute simplicity and beauty.

While we were at the School, a beautiful American woman approached us and asked if my name was Ivonne. When I answered that it was, she ran over to hug me with such love! Her face radiated with joy and devotion, and her smile was shining. For many years, she was a disciple of Swami Muktananda and, when he had his *Mahasamadhi*, she continued her spiritual path under the guidance of Swami Nityananda.

She kindly took us to the place where Nityananda would be arriving to do the program of the day for Saraswati—the goddess of knowledge and music. A huge fire (*yajna*) blazed in the room for an ancient ceremony where the Brahmin priests offered holy substances while chanting Vedic mantras.

Many people sat on the floor, waiting for Swamiji's arrival. When Nityananda walked into the room, my heart opened up even more. He was a tall man with an enormous [11]rudrashka mala hanging around his neck. In his orange robes, with a huge smile, he sat down and began chanting the thousand names of the Divine as Mother.

Wow. It was amazing and intense—the fire burning, the smoke, the chanting. I had only one thought in mind: purification. People were coughing from the smoke and wearing handkerchiefs around their mouths to breathe. I had no trouble with that. Everything was purifying. I just felt like chanting (even if I didn't know the language), singing, and dancing for two hours.

My heart was opened, my mind was being purified, and then the moment came when I felt in my heart that "this" is my idea of a guru. Nityananda began chanting a mantra with such devotion, rhythm, and passion for the goddess! I just chanted and chanted along with everyone. People became ecstatic; the energy generated was of total celebration, similar to fans of pop artists such as Madonna. People just go crazy singing her songs at concerts. Here the same mood was happening, except the songs were to Saraswati. It was pure ecstatic bliss.

After the chanting, the moment of *darshan* came. To be honest, I had butterflies about meeting Swami Nityananda. I had heard so many things about him from friends and my ex-teacher but, somehow in the celebration of the moment, all of that was forgotten. We lined up to take our turn to greet the guru. A beautiful Australian woman, Claire, kindly assisted us and presented us to Nityananda. He sat in the right-hand corner of the room, at one side of the sweet and loving Deviani (his personal assistant), who played the harmonium (an Indian classical instrument, which has forty-two black-and-white keys that corresponds to the equal temperament of Western music) in a beautiful way. She treated us with such love and warmth. She later hugged me and acknowledged our mutual contact, Delia, for her impeccability in words, thoughts, and deeds. Deviani told

---

11. *Rudra* means Shiva and *Aksh* means eye. Therefore, it is said that only those who see Shiva as the Creator can wear this auspicious prayer bead. Rudraksha is nature's gift to mankind. Rudra is the name of Lord Shiva. Aksha also means 'tear'. It is said that the plant of Rudraksha is originated from the teardrops of Lord Shiva. As per the Vedic scriptures, Rudraksha can nullify the effects of malefic planets to a great extent. No other necklace or bead is so auspicious and powerful as a Rudraksha. If worn with certain precautions, in general, the wearer of Rudraksha is blessed with prosperity, peace, and health. http://www.celextel.com/products/rudraksha_malas.htm

me that she had heard many stories about me and my husband, but with a smile she made a gesture that said, *now* is all that matters!

Our turn came, and we found ourselves at the feet of the guru. I experienced a child-like happiness and simplicity. I was so excited that even my rehearsed words disappeared from my mind. His energy, the three hours of chanting, and the Vedic Yajna ceremony just blew me away. We gave him some gifts that we brought from Mexico, and then we left the room.

Outside a celebration was going on with musicians dressed in traditional Indian costumes. In the center of the yard was a circle where people were gathered to do a special dance. They invited me to participate. When they asked, "Would you...?" I was already in the circle! It was such a beautiful experience—the energy and the dancing! Almost all the people held hands and began dancing together in certain rhythm and with special feet movement traditional to the dance, circling around the open space with the sky as a witness. Nityananda watched, and the starry night became one of the most memorable India experiences for me. While dancing, I felt the motivation and love to share more joy with many others. What a blessing to be of service, don't you think? What a blessing to be alive!

The group visit to Mahamandaleshwar Swami Nityananda, who continues the spiritual work of his guru, Baba Muktananda, continuing the lineage of Siddha gurus, enlightened masters, immersed in consciousness.
© Mastery Life A.C

# 4

# *Babaji Nagaraj, the Sacred Feet Experience*

All praise be to thy lotus feet,
While my heart is the sacred offering to your hands.

*~ Ivonne Delaflor*

# Rishikesh and the Mystery of Babaji
## October 4

A Moment's Good Company Will Enable
Human Beings to Cross the Worldly Ocean.
~ *Swami Shankarananda Giri*

At 4 AM we got out of bed, took a bath, and practiced some Yoga, and in an hour we were standing in the lobby ready to go for our five-hour drive. Unfortunately, Mr. Rana could not drive us this day. A young man with a very white smiley grin took us. He was also the one who had driven us to Greenfield's School to meet Nityananda. When I had asked him the night before if he would be the one driving us to Rishikesh, he said, "No…I am tired." But destiny had other plans for him. He was the one chosen by Mr. Joseph to take us. (See? Sometimes you don't get what you want, but you get what you need!)

Along the way, we made many stops. There was a car accident; there were many cows crossing the road; a road was closed and we had to find another route—everything directed our driver to go more slowly. This time I was sitting in the front seat with the driver. I was on his left because in India, like in many parts of Europe, the driver sits on the right side of the car. My friends went to sleep, and the driving became surreal. It was like being inside a computer game, and I was driving along with the driver!

I witnessed the deep orange-red sunrise painting the clouds with its presence and felt the nurturing warmth of it, recognizing the beauty and uniqueness of each moment. During all of our traveling by plane, I was able to see both the sunrise and sunset…different…special. The road was of such magnificence, the trees at the side roads, the cars driving fast, the colors of the newborn morning…and once I had decided to tell God that he should be the one driving us, I relaxed and enjoyed the rest of the adventure to Rishikesh.

We made a stop after a few hours at a small restaurant for my friends to have breakfast and for the driver to drink some coffee. He really needed it! I couldn't eat at all. I just felt like fasting and drinking water, which included all sorts of strange supplementation, from chlorophyll drops to liquid oxygen. I felt very quiet and attentive to the signs. No words today.

Outside the restaurant, a man was selling magazines and newspapers, but one little book called my attention. It was an old book written by another guru, Osho (also known as Rajneesh). Osho was my first "encounter" with a spiritual teacher from India. My husband gave me some tapes of talks and a book written by him when we first met. I liked him. What was called to my attention was the title of the book, *Few Words by a Man of No Words*. Bingo! Perfect for what I was thinking. By now, all messages and all pictures of any guru manifesting were as alive as I was. I felt Osho's energy strongly, and I bought the book. Throughout our drive, I read beautiful teachings from him that were perfect for the moment. Osho used to say that we should never worry about anything. We should remain open in the now with no desire, just be in the celebration of the now.

We continued our journey; my friends rested for a while again. I was just owl-eyed in wonder! I felt something powerful but sharp. I didn't know what it was, but I was very attentive. The view of the old road was beautiful. I opened the window to feel the air. The wind began blowing in a particularly intense fashion. The trees seemed to be dancing with the wind.

We passed Haridwar and saw many orange-robed *sannyasins* (Hindu monks who renounced the world in order to realize God) walking by. Many ashrams fill that small city, and many renunciants and devotees live there. A small sign caught my attention: *Celebrating the Mahasamadhi of Anandamayi Ma's*. It was such a small sign that I wondered why would I turn to read it. Why was it in English? Why not? Ha!

Seven years ago, I was at my husband's house in Cuernavaca. We went to spend a weekend there, and I took my little dog Marla, a Yorkshire terrier, with me. Marla was used to sleeping with me, but my husband didn't like that. She wouldn't stop barking, too, and that was bothering him. I decided to take my dog to a guestroom and sat down on the bed. Marla climbed up and slipped under the sheets. I was very tired but awake and sleepy. I reached my hand down under the sheets and touched someone else's hand!

In my sleepiness, I did not freak out. I walked my hand up the bed and felt a pregnant belly. I knew it was not mine. I continued to move my hand up the bed. When I opened my eyes, I saw a beautiful Indian woman lying on the bed. She was smiling at me and caressing my arm. In my sleepy voice I said to her, "Please take care of my dog and make sure she doesn't bark any more." The woman smiled.

Immediately I realized what was happening—this was a vision on a different dimension. The unknown took over, and I became afraid. I jumped and ran toward the bedroom where my husband was. I jumped in bed with him and covered myself with the sheets like a frightened little child. What had just happened?

Years later, when I met one of my beloved Yoga teachers, Bhavani, she brought me pictures of all the mystics and a book, *Autobiography of a Yogi*. A thrill covered my being when I opened it to read about Yogananda's encounter with Ananda Maya Ma. I researched about her and found a picture of her. She was the same person I had seen in the guestroom in Cuernavaca that day! This little sign about her [1]*Mahasamadhi* helped me to remember that day and her energy was palpable in my heart again.

A huge rocky mountain rose behind other mountains covered with snow. I asked the driver what those were, and he replied, "The Himalayas!" Wow and mega wow! In my wildest dreams I never imagined seeing the Himalayas in person. And although I had just a peek at them, I felt very happy and fulfilled for that moment—like when I was a child and waited for Santa Claus's presents under the tree every Christmas. That was enough for me.

We were very close to Rishikesh now. After six hours we had finally arrived. I asked the driver where he was going to take us, assuming that there was a plan. Every other time our driver had directions, meetings had been arranged prior to our arrival, and so on. Yet he answered, "I don't know where to go." I asked again, "You didn't receive any instructions?" He said, "No." He then told us that he would take us to the tourist parts of the city to see the Ganges and then we would go back to Delhi. He was tired. My antennas were vibrating differently, however.

I began directing the driver uphill. I told him I wanted to go up, close to the mountains. The old streets were very narrow. The small city was crowded. Rishikesh is considered a very spiritual sacred place. It is near the mouth of the Ganges, the holy river, which is said to have emanated from Lord Shiva's hair.[2] Situated in the Indian state of Uttaranchal, Rishikesh is a very important Hindu pilgrimage site. There also are a number of ashrams and temples that give the entire place a spiritual feeling. The ceaseless flow of the river, regarded as Goddess Ganga, adds to the beauty and the purity of the place. Along the river, the area is filled with thick green forests in the all-mountainous region. The entire area falls on the Garhwal region of Northern India. Hordes of sadhus (sages) come to this place every year in search of salvation. We continued driving uphill.

---

1.   According to Hinduism, Mahasamadhi—also spelled Maha Samadhi—is the final conscious abandoning of the physical body. It is a God-illumined master's consciousness exiting from the body at the time of physical death—the Great Liberation. To achieve Mahasamadhi, all karma must be completed—the individual having achieved self-awareness or soul realization. http://www.crystalinks. com/mahasamadhi.html

2.   www.indianvisit.com

Our driver was getting more and more irritated because he was tired. Suddenly he announced, "I am taking you to the tourist area." I literally screamed back, "Stop here!"

He reversed the car a little bit, and we went inside a very humble ashram, the Kriya Yoga Ashram of Rishikesh. Construction workers were busy, yet I knew in my heart that we were in the right place. We went inside. Our driver parked, and a young swami came out. When I approached to greet him, I automatically said, "I wish to see Babaji."

He replied, "*Ha ha ha ha ha*. Are you ready? One must be prepared to meet Babaji. He is in Delhi right now."

I told him, "But I know he can move his body as he wishes." The swami agreed with me, and then I introduced myself.

He was so smiley. He invited us inside the office where hanging on the wall was a picture of his guru, [3]Swami Shankarananda Giri. The young swami, Muktananda, was a delight. (Appropriate, isn't it?) He served us tea and cookies. I ended my fast. He told us that his teacher had just left for Delhi that morning and would be back the next day. Then he spontaneously gave me a gift of a book written by his teacher, *Bringing the Inner God to Life*, based on the Patanjali Yoga Sutras.

I felt a deep connection of love and joy with Muktananda. His smile was as white as the Himalayas themselves! Then he gave gifts to all my friends, too. We shared our story about how we arrived there—guided by magic and signs along the way. He told us that one hour before our "unannounced" arrival, he was supposed to go to the market to do some grocery shopping for the ashram, but his little jitney wouldn't start. He had tried for almost an hour, but as soon as we drove up, his car started! He was about to drive off but hospitality dictated that he stay with us.

Muktananda then invited us to the meditation room. We were very grateful and felt very blessed by his presence and the evident energy of Babaji. When we entered the meditation room, my legs became like Jell-O. I immediately sat down in lotus position in front of the largest picture of Sri Yukteswar (Paramahansa Yogananda's guru) I've ever seen. At his left was an enormous picture of Swami

---

3.   Swami Shankarananda Giri has been teaching Kriya Yoga techniques in India since 1974 and in Europe since 1978. He has also inherited the astrological system called Cosmic Astrology from his master Swami Narayana Giri (Prabhujee). This system was established by Sri Yukteswar. http://www.kriya-yoga.com/

Yogananda and another saint named Bhabu. On his right was a photo of Babaji and Shankarananda Giri, his spiritual heir.

Muktananda, Amenanda, and Govinda in Rishikesh at the Kriya Yoga
Ashram © Mastery Life A.C

I was blown away (or should I say, blown within) by the pictures and by the energy of the ashram. I was actually sitting in front of the image of Sri Yukteswar, someone to whom I've always felt very connected. We were there in the meditation room of the Kriya Yoga Ashram, guided by spirit and trusting in the magic of God.

We all began spontaneously meditating. Not much effort was needed to quiet the mind. The energy was so intense that the mind quieted itself. Nothing to do; no distractions—just natural focus. My breathing began to be very subtle...quiet. ...I was in complete peace. This time there were no sensational events...no colorful realities. It was just this moment...peace. No thoughts...no time. I heard someone walking into the room and the sound of the door closing. At the same time I had a vision of Sri Yukteswar pouring water on my head and caressing it with such love. The footsteps now were getting closer. I was just listening. I felt very peaceful...feeling at home...inside myself...in the depths of my soul.

Then something or someone whispered to me. I can only think it was the wind. The whispering voice said, "Open your eyes." I opened them just halfway. My eyes were still looking inward. Looking out I saw, literally, right in front of me, a pair of beautiful feet. Barefoot, the skin was brown and flowers had been placed on them. I was struck speechless! I did not open my eyes any more. I was paralyzed. In front of me was no literal space for someone to stand on. Then I heard the whispered voice saying, "Babaji." Shivers covered my body. I wept tears of gratitude.

Ahhhhh, I said to myself, I will not open my eyes for if I see you in your totality, I might never want to go back to the West. Then the voice said, "The time will come." I opened my eyes, and what had seemed a few brief minutes of meditation had been actually nearly forty minutes.

The peaceful, relaxed, and radiant faces of my friends were enlightened. After the meditation, the young Muktananda said, "I think you are ready for the Kriya Yoga initiation. Come next year, you will stay here and be initiated." I just smiled and felt peace and gratitude bigger than the Himalayas themselves!

But, you may ask, who is Babaji?

The group after the experience of
the Divine Shaktipat of Mahavatar Babaji.
At the Kriya Yoga Ashram with Muktananda © Mastery Life A.C

# Who is Babaji?

When we deliberately leave the safety of the shore of our lives,
we surrender to the mystery beyond our intent.
~ *Ann Linnea*

After I read the book, *The Initiation,* and spontaneously experienced Divine states of prema and visions of Babaji, my mind began asking, *but who is this Babaji?*

I wrote to Prema Baba Swamiji with this question, and he responded through an E-mail to me that as with all things sacred, there is always an exoteric and esoteric meaning. The meaning in English for Babaji is "Venerable Father." The word Baba is similar to the word Abba used by Jesus to praise God, which means Divine Father and Mother. Prema Baba explained to me that the esoteric meaning for the word Babaji is in truth, a prayer. It is the answer to all prayers when pronounced with grand respect and reverence. He told me that Babaji is a very old being with the ability of regeneration. He also is king of the serpent people, known as Nagas in South America. It is believed that Babaji initiated both [4]Patanjali and [5]Shankaracharya.

The amazing stories of those who have had the experience of seeing the Divine presence of Babaji seemed unreal to me...until the moment that the story became a reality! Many beliefs dropped away, and I am sure they will keep on dropping constantly from our minds.

Who is Babaji? More than a mystery of the highest order for me, Babaji became an adventure that has just begun.

After the blessed experience inside the Kriya Yoga Ashram, it was time to say farewell, but we now had a longing to bring Muktananda with us back to Mexico. In awe, we experienced a shivering humbleness that we had never experienced before!

---

4.  Patanjali: Founder of the system of Yoga and author of the Yoga Sutras, the ancient text that establishes the practice and philosophy of Yoga. www.kofibusia.com/Yoga/Pages/PatanjaliBiography.html

5.  Shankaracharya is the first among the three acharyas who reformed Hindu religion by giving their own interpretation to the ancient sacred texts. At the time, the Vedic texts, which have come down to Indians through the ages and only orally studied, were the monopoly of a certain class. This knowledge was known as shruti, or learning by careful listening. http://www.kamat.com/indica/faiths/bhakti/shankaracharya.htm

We left the ashram and headed toward the street market. Our driver spoke with a friend of his who was a guide. We hired him to walk us through Rishikesh. The entire city was celebrating the Goddess Durga. Everyone was chanting. We stopped by one temple to see an enormous Shiva lingam. People would circumambulate around it. I began doing the ritual when a *sannyasin* gestured to me. "This way, please." He walked me to a room where a very old guru—he must have been seventy years old—was lying on a bed. He was in total bliss, and my mind again stopped. His drunkenness in God was contagious. No one dared to speak to the guru, yet I decided to tell him how happy I felt. Our guide was surprised. He was not expecting this. I shared with him what I was feeling, and the old man smiled even more. He was drunk with Divine Love. Later I came to know that his name was Shankaracharya.

We visited a Vishnu temple and then walked down the rocky hill to meet the holy Ganges. On our way down, a calf got close to me for a caress. It was a beautiful moment. We walked over the river on a long bridge that seemed to be as fragile as the clear water of the river itself, crowded by people crossing from one side of the river to the other. The Ganges was blessing us with its presence! The green-and-white mountains surrounded us; a crowd of people walked with us.

The view was heavenly and breathtaking. All we could see was the natural and organic beauty, the people dressed in their festive colors, the mountains, the sound of endless chants and prayers…everything seemed like a perfect color for the divine painting. We took off our shoes and walked into the clear river where the water was cold but relaxing. The sparkling of silver gave it a special shine. Wherever we looked there was beauty: our feet in the Ganges, Babaji, the cow, my friends, love. Isn't God grand?

At the river, my friends shared their stories about being in the meditation room. All of them had heard someone enter the room as I did. Govinda felt a presence breathing close to him. Devananda felt a hand placed on her right shoulder, and she saw Yogananda. Bhakti said she was peaceful and attentive and felt that something special was happening. Alex, my dear Akshmilanandaji, had an experience in which a cloud manifested for him, and Babaji took him inside of it.

After a few moments at the Ganges, we quietly walked back to the market. We stopped to buy some mala beads, and Alex contacted a Vedic astrologer. He had wanted to meet at least one during our journey. Then, we found fantastic food in a two-story restaurant with plastic dinner tables but that had a view of the mountains…the wind…the sun…and the magnificent Ganges.

Later than expected, we started on our way back toward Delhi. This time, I didn't choose the front seat. I gave Alex the opportunity to drive along with the driver. Faith and trust were still the main tools we needed for India's driving lessons. On our return trip, a car got so close to us that I swear it was like in the movies! I was so grateful that our driver had very good reflexes!

The group in the Ganges in Rishikesh, bathing their feet after receiving
the blessing of the materialization of the sacred feet of Mahavatar Babaji
© Mastery Life A.C

# 5

## *The Cherry on the Cake*

What is there that is not perfect in creation?
For all cycles are created by your Divine presence,
and the experience of completion
is like a kiss from the sun.

*~ Ivonne Delaflor*

# Until Next Time
## The Blessed Reencounter with My Little Goo-roos
## October 5

It is not for him to pride himself with loveth his own country,
but rather for him who loveth the whole world.
The earth is but one country and mankind its citizens.
~ *Bahá'u'lláh*

I woke up at the hotel later than usual. I had gone to sleep at 3 AM from packing and the excitement of traveling home. I did my Yoga practice as usual and then had breakfast by myself. We checked out and had a wonderful last conversation with the people there. Since our flight was not until 10 PM, we left our bags at the hotel. Our driver picked us up, and we headed toward the Lotus Temple, the Baha'i house of worship. The shape of the architecture is a lotus flower. The petals are made of white concrete covered in white Greek marble panels. The lotus represents purity, worship, and religion. There are seven temples like this one in different parts of the world. Each has its distinctive design; each invites people of all religions and races to worship the Creator of the Universe and to express the love between God and man. The temple itself is well organized. There are no Hindu, Buddhist, or Christian deities inside, however. It was built for all religions to worship without discrimination.

The Basic Baha'i principles are:

- The oneness of mankind
- Independent investigation of Truth
- The common foundation of all religions
- The essential harmony of science and religion
- Equality of men and women
- Elimination of prejudice of all kinds
- Universal compulsory education
- Universal peace

Inside the temple, the only thing requested is silence. The intention of the temple is for meditation, and that is what we did. Once again I had a very profound experience. Suddenly no one was around. The memory of being in Bangkok six years ago came back to me. I was inside the crowded Golden Palace meditating in the Emerald Buddha Temple. Years ago I didn't have a lot of programming regarding meditation. I had a spontaneous experience of no space, no time, and no one around. In Bangkok, when I opened my eyes I remembered asking, "Where am I?" This time, I had the same sensation but instead of a question, an affirmation arose: I am here.

Swami Amenanda at the Lotus Temple, where the experience of *No Time* became more palpable during meditation. © Mastery Life A.C

After the meditation, we went for lunch and then to Swami Nityananda's house. There the beautiful Deviani received us with such warmth. We took off our shoes and went up the stairs to the living room. We sat on the floor, and Nityananda came in. We had a privileged two-hour talk with him, sharing stories. He gave us guidance regarding raising children consciously, without TVs or excessive amount of toys. His wisdom, simplicity, and beauty will stay in my heart forever.

Something interesting happened, though. I was personally attracted to his feet! I just felt drawn to massage them or to sit by them. Yep, the "Feet of the Guru" experience. It had never happened to me before. I'd heard many stories about worshiping at the feet of a guru but, to be honest, I'd never been attracted to vow to feet! Internally, I was laughing a lot. Nityananda was very attentive and listening to all we said. He offered us candy that tasted delicious!

We all wanted him to come to Cancun, and he replied, "Come first to New York." We took a picture with him, and I sat close to his feet. The conversation continued for a while, and then the time came for us to leave. We were grateful for the guidance he gave us, for the humbleness he demonstrated to us, and for the honor to have spent two precious hours with him—that was the cherry on the cake!

Can you believe we had last minute shopping to do? A candy store this time. Then to the hotel to pick up our luggage, and at 11 PM we were at the airport. Everyone went through customs smoothly but, when my turn arrived, they didn't want to let me through. I didn't know that I needed to show my United States visa. When I finally understood, an officer came to look at it and said everything was in order. I felt such relief!

We waited for almost three hours, and at 2 AM on October 6 we boarded the plane for a nine-hour flight to Frankfurt. This time I did sleep. All I could think about was the moment where I would kiss my most important gurus again—my daughter Alhia and Christian, my beloved son.

We arrived in Germany, took some pictures, chatted for a while, and then boarded the second airplane to Florida. Again, I watched the sunset through the window. The stewardess was serving with such love and practicing her Spanish with me. My heart beat as rapidly as the first time I got on the plane to India. Another adventure had begun—seeing my children again, integrating the experience of India, and sharing more love with everyone.

When we arrived in Florida, I was going to pick up my children who had been traveling. My friends were continuing on to Cancun. We said farewell in a most intimate way because now we were connected for eternity. We had shared something that not even words could express.

When we came out of the gate, the first person I saw was Christian. He was sleeping in his stroller, and Mariela, his nanny, was with him. I kissed him, and he opened his eyes. He blinked for a bit and then he cried, letting me know in his own language how much he had missed me. I carried him in my arms. Then I saw my daughter, Alhia. I swear that what I feel with my children is more than a journey; it is 10,000 billion of *Indias* all together. My children's love and their smiles...their possibilities to be who they are is such a pure divine blessing. It is magic like no other.

I was home. The quote I used to hear about *home is where the heart is* was and is now a reality for me. No matter where I go, or how many times I move from one house to another—we have moved nine times already—I always carry my home wherever I go. I meet special beings everywhere. There is always someone to help, someone to learn from, new experiences to live, and my dear friend the sunset always comes along with me.

Upon my return, I gave my children the tape of the *Bhagavad-Gita.* They have been delighted with it. I even catch my daughter playing it alone in her room, repeating spontaneously, "I am Brahma."

These days, India keeps manifesting for me—a neighbor from India; the Hindu doctor who attended to my daughter from a complication she experienced during surgery; the Rasmani Ring; my friend Satprem; people spontaneously inviting me to Hindu dances; the Ayurvedic Center. The presence and reverberation of India is a continuous reminder. Suddenly I see India everywhere. As when I was pregnant, all of a sudden I became aware of how many pregnant women were around! Now I am aware of the presence of India in the world, in my world. India is a beautiful entity...its jasmine fragrance...its food is divine nectar...so similar to magical Mexico in many ways.

Regarding the message about writing the book, *Babaji Speaks to the Parents of the World,* to be honest, I haven't started with that yet. I am waiting for a sign...perhaps another moment. I will just wait; maybe it is not for me to actually write the book. One thing I am sure of, though, I will be very attentive.

It is now time to bring to completion this narration with a dialogue I had with my daughter just after my return. In the meantime, thank you for reading these words. They are only five percent of the experience of India that mere words could never really convey. You've traveled along with me through India's mysticism and the presence of Divine Love. I wish you nothing but more of who you already are. Stay in love…create more peace…and have a wonderful journey: *a journey of a lifetime.*

Alhia: "Mommy, you look sad…why?"
Ivonne: "I was just missing India"
Alhia: "No Mommy! Don't do that!"
Ivonne: "Why, Baby?"
Alhia: "Because I want you to stay here with me…In your body
and your head."
Ivonne: (shedding a small tear) "Thank you, thank you…."

# One year later

Good people come to worship me for different reasons.
Some come to the spiritual life because of suffering;
Some in order to understand life; some come through
a desire to achieve life's purpose,
and some come who are men and women of wisdom.
Unwavering in devotion, always united with me, the man or woman of wisdom
surpasses all the others. To them I am the dearest beloved,
and they are very dear to me. All those who follow the spiritual path are blessed.
But the wise who are always established in union, for whom there is no higher
goal than me, may be regarded as my very Self.
~ Bhagavad Gita *7:16–18*

The experience we had in India keeps surprising me. Nothing has changed and
yet everything has evolved. India is powerful and sacred. Yet, the entire world is,
too. The *leelas* keep manifesting as they were meant to. I continue encountering
beautiful beings devoted to serving others—Western yogis who serve with their
beliefs and kind hearts and work for all who match their own vibration.

The experience we had with Mahavatar Babaji was an awakening itself. We all
are quiet from it, watching our thoughts of self-limitations and useless beliefs
dropping away in the process. Many relationships came to completion after
India, and others were reconnected. It is the forever dance of polarities. My contact with my first meditation teacher emerged again with an experience of deepest
gratitude.

Babaji's message is yet to be awakened and yet…it has already. I have moved
away from Cancun and also from self-imposed attitudes and behaviors. I live in
the mountains now, focused on my children, and assisting whenever the opportunity manifests itself, to whomever I can, in whatever way possible.

I must confess that the mystery of Babaji and what happened almost at the
end (or shall I say the beginning?) of our journey will live in our multidimensionality forever. I sometimes indulge in a question: Was it real?

I often remind myself of that day, October 5, 2003. The Navaratri was almost
complete. I was traveling with my devotional friends for eight hours in a little car
toward Rishikesh, following the signs of the heart of a dream. I was following the
magic that had beautifully haunted me in the most positive ways since I have
memory of my own childhood. Then a three-dimensional shiver appeared as I
viewed the Himalayas!

All my traveling and all of my experiences cannot compare with what happened in—what? Was it two hours? Was it just forty-five minutes? Time ceased to exist that day...this day. Was it real?

The excitement, the blindness, the transmission—how could it happen for a Western mind? Why me? I am a mother, a sinner, a human being...a dreamer of peace...a true extremist in the path of love. Why me? What was the reason? These questions have no answers, and they never will.

It is now nine months after that day. India...Rishikesh...the Kriya Yoga Ashram. It was the most humble place we visited in my heart's pilgrimage to India.

I wrote my experience in this book to share with you, dear reader. I offer written pages of the experience that happened. My heart tells me it deserves more...even more than mere spoken or written words. Yet, "the more" is silent...only creating a sound for those who really can listen. How could it be that one day before returning to my family, to the known, to the Western world, that the real adventure manifested? It happened, in front of our human eyes—wide-open, with five witnesses who, like me, veiled the experience with distractions, beliefs, and advice from others.

Was it real? The bhakti tears; the shivers are intensifying. All of this the mind is trying to avoid.

After so many months I actually feel closer to India and spontaneously I witness myself listening to an inner Japa:

*OM NAMAH SHIVAYA,*
*SHIVAYA NAMAHA...*
*OM NAMAH SHIVAYA,*
*SHIVAYA NAMAHA...OM*
*NAMAH SHIVAYA,*
*SHIVAYA NAMAHA*
...over and over again.

I look at the pictures that Swami Govinda took inside the Kriya Yoga Ashram. I see a picture of Sri Yukteswar, Lahiri Mahasaya, Bhabu, Yogananda, Swami Shankarananda Giri, and Sri Babaji. I was at the feet of what seemed to be the only photograph that somehow was sprouting inside my heart. The images became doors for the avatars to come and grace us with their living presence.

What happened that day? Where did time go? I remember those footsteps. There was a carpet, and the sound was a bare foot making a strong and intense step. The wind was blowing inside of a closed room! Where did that voice come from? Was it the mind? Does it really matter? Death became nonexistent and, in that moment, the appreciation for what is eternal—Life—gave birth to no words. It awakened in others so much to project...to say...to direct...to think...yet I only observed...as I do now.

I came back from India with so many questions. I looked for those whom I thought might assist me with some guidance or information here in the West. One by one they demonstrated I should not ask or I should just remain in silent contemplation. Some couldn't answer me. Others did not believe. Still others were cautious for their own feelings and beliefs were at stake.

My friends and I are keeping India now as an esoteric and magical memory. Yet, there is an energy that is not letting us forget. It is stronger than our own minds...even stronger than the heart. It is empty of any explanation and full of silent answers.

India called us. We had no plans to go there. We were invited by the Divine. Everything unfolded so magically, so "Soulmately"...so...perfectly. It was miraculous.

Currently, I spend my days practicing my karma Yoga, serving my children, my husband, and friends with my heart. Being quiet is a most natural state. I am a hermit in the mountains who loves shopping, who makes mistakes, meditates, and has an amazing trust and passion for life and love.

I thought the memory of India was already a memory; I thought I had agreed with my mind and other people's minds that the experience was just a delusion or something not necessary to remember. The ego dances once in a while, I know. The dance of illusion comes and goes, but the experience that happened without labeling concepts is rebirthing itself constantly. One by one, the idols have dropped themselves from the illusory altar I created in my mind for them. Yet, the space they leave is one of love and possibilities.

Then...the memory returns. The feet that materialized and a name *Babaji, Babaji, Babaji*. It was the perfect setting...the perfect place. Mother India just speaks silently: *Go back home.*

There is no thirst for searching, and yet the longing of the Divine presence will remain always in our hearts. The world is as it is. No matter how grand the experience might look, there is nothing grander than life itself. Breathing is free...and it is a magical experience to recognize it. The breath carries its own traveling mood, its own journey.

We all have had a diversity of experiences and have been watching the response of others regarding it. We keep on evolving and making choices that we believe assist us to remain as one with God. My beautiful friends now are creating the manifestation of a spiritual community in Cancun, and the creation of a temple for all religions that was donated to us by a beautiful soul. Evolution never stops. Enlightenment is for everyone.

India is here and everywhere...and so is the world. Why shall we name the experience with any label whatsoever? The experience is "Now" and the adventure, the mysticism, the real Guru and the best journey...begins with love. It is only love.

Know that if you love...you are already blessed. Remember that while loving, you are truly experiencing a real journey of a lifetime.

So be it.

Om Namah Shivaya

# *About the Author*

Ivonne Delaflor, author, teacher, and spiritual practitioner, is a certified Parent Talk trainer and Director of the Parent Talk System in Mexico. As a strong supporter of conscious evolution and God's Realization for all children of the world, Ivonne founded the Mastery Life, a nonprofit organization based in Mexico in 2002, whose main intention is to share conscious tools with fellow human beings—especially the tools that can assist in the wonderful journey of parenthood to guide children to their full potential as blessed human beings.

Called by her friends as a modern female saint for her active work with parents and children at the orphanage, *La Casita de Cancun*, she is a survivor of a near-death experience at the age of eighteen that turned her life into a spiritual quest. She began to meet with recognized spiritual teachers worldwide and today shares her passion through offering free workshops and intuitive wisdom in respecting and allowing both children and adults to be who they really are.

Ivonne is the creator of the twelve-module workshop, *Rediscovering Yourself through Your Personal Power*. She is also the author of *Your Soulmate Called God, La Maestria de La Vida* published in Mexico, *The Positive Child through the Language of Love,* and *Mastering Life,* which are available at www.iuniverse.com, www.amazon.com, and major bookstores. She is currently working on a workbook entitled, *Practical Exercises for the Positive Child for Body, Mind, and Spirit,* the profits of which will go to the orphanage La Casita de Cancun. She also is co-authoring a book for children that will be donated to the Waldorf School of Santa Barbara, California. She recently published the book INVITATION TO LOVE, dictated through automatic writing to her by Sri Babaji Nagaraj, available at www.amazon.com and www.iuniverse.com.

Ivonne conducts regular free workshops in Cancun, and through her *Mastery Life Organization* assists spiritual teachers such as Doreen Virtue, Chick Moorman, Alan Cohen, and many others to share their wisdom in raising the consciousness and awareness that through love children will evolve and teach us their peaceful ways.

One hundred percent of the profits of this book will be donated to the Bhaktivedanta Ashram & Bhaktivedanta International Charities (http://www.

foodrelief.org) for the creation of an orphanage for the children affected by the disaster caused by a tsunami in South India in 2004.

Ivonne currently lives with her husband and her two children in California. You may contact her through her website: http://www.masterylife.com/ or you can send an e-mail to admin@masterylife.com.

# Glossary of Sanskrit Terms

Agni—"Fire;" the God Fire.

Amrita—"Immortal;" nectar.

Arati—A worship ceremony, the "waving of the light."

Ashram—A religious center started by or dedicated to a saint.

Avatar—"Descent, incarnation;" usually denotes one of the ten incarnations of Vishnu.

Bhagavad Gita—"Song of God;" a major Hindu scripture and a chapter from the Mahabharata that contains Krishna's teaching on realizing God.

Bhajan—Devotional song.

Bhakti—Religious or spiritual devotion; love.

Brahma—God in the aspect of Creator of the universe; one of the Hindu trinity.

Brahman—A member of the highest, priestly class in Hindu society.

Chai—tea.

Chapatti—Unleavened flat bread.

Darshan—The blessing of seeing and being in the presence of a saint or holy Master.

Deva—"Deity" or celestial being.

Dosha—In the Ayurvedic system, the "three humors:" vata, pitta, and kapha.

Ganesha—The elephant-headed god, son of Shiva and Uma.

Garuda—A mythical bird that is half-man and half-beast associated with tremendous speed and power.

Gopi—A female devotee of Krishna.

Hanuman—The monkey king of the Ramayana, the archetype of the selfless devotee.

Kali—The "dark" Hindu goddess who destroys illusions.

Kum kum—A mark, usually a dot, made from red turmeric or colored powder on the "third eye" (ajna).

Leela (or lila)—"Cosmic play" of the Divine.

Lingam—Phallic symbol of Shiva.

Mahasamadhi—"Great absorption;" a saint's final passing to God at the time of his or her physical death.

Malas—Prayer beads.

Mandir—A Hindu temple.

Math—A religious center, an ashram, or a monastery.

Maya—"Cosmic illusion;" the divine power of illusion.

Mudra—A positioning of the hand or body in a particular way to channel one's energy and consciousness.

Namaskar, Namaste—Salutation, "I bow to God in you."

Om—The key manta of Hinduism, symbolizing the Absolute.

Prana—"Breath" or life force.

Prasad—Food eaten after it has first been offered to God or to a saint.

Puja—A ritual veneration of a deity or guru.

*Pujari*—A temple priest.

Radha—Krishna's beloved and devotee.

Ravana—The demon king who abducted Sita, Rama's wife. He was later killed by Rama. The story is told in the Ramayana.

Rishi—An ancient sage.

Rudraksh or Rudraksha—A round seed that is sacred to Lord Shiva, used in rosaries or prayer beads.

Samadhi—A state of profound or one-pointed consciousness.

Sannyasin—Religious mendicant.

Shakti—The feminine aspect of the Divine; energy or power.

Shiva (or Siva)—God in the aspect of destroyer; one of the Hindu trinity.

Siddha—An "accomplished one."

Tilak—A mark of auspiciousness put on the forehead with sandalwood paste, sacred ashes, or kum kum.

Vishnu—God in the aspect of the maintainer of the universe; one of the Hindu trinity.

Yajna—"Sacrifice;" a Vedic fire ritual.

# Contact Information

Mastery Life A.C
www.masterylife.com
For Spanish Language: Bhaktiananda@masterylife.com
Govinda@masterylife.com

Alex Slucki
Swami Aksmilanandaji
www.huellasdeluz.com
swamiakshmilandaji@masterylife.com

*The Initiation*
www.innerocean.com
www.amazon.com

Sivashankar Baba
4/164, Ellaiamman Koil Street,
Neelankarai, Madras
Tamil Nadu, Pin-600041
INDIA
Tel: +91-44-4491050, 4491060.
smrtchna@giasmd01.vsnl.net.in
www.samratchana.org

Ramakrishna Mat
www.ramakrishna.org

Angena
Tourist guide
Chennai 600028 South India
Tel: 493 61 68

Govind Joshi
Tourist guide
Agra, Taj Mahal
Tel: 0091562 24 01 1033
Joshi_Govin@yahoo.com.in

Amma's Organization
www.amritapuri.org
www.amma.org

Mahamandaleshwar Swami Nityananda
www.shantimandir.com

Sathya Sai Baba
www.sathyasai.org

Sri Aurobindo Ashram, New Delhi
aurobindo@vsnl.com

Baha'i House of Worship
Lotus Temple
www.bahaindia.org